Prophet of Reunion

Prophet of Reunion
The Life of Paul of Graymoor

CHARLES ANGELL, S.A.
CHARLES LaFONTAINE, S.A.

With an Introduction by
*James Stuart Wetmore, Suffragan Bishop
of the Episcopal Diocese of New York*

A CROSSROAD BOOK
The Seabury Press · New York

The Seabury Press
815 Second Avenue
New York, N.Y. 10017

Copyright © 1975 by The Seabury Press, Inc.
Designed by Lynn Braswell
Printed in the United States of America

LIBRARY OF CONGRESS CATALOGING IN PUBLICATION DATA

Angell, Charles.
Prophet of reunion.

"A Crossroad book."
1. Paul James Francis, Father, 1863–1940.
I. LaFontaine, Charles, joint author. II. Title.
BX4705.P3842A8   248′.242′0924 [B]   74–32239
ISBN 0–8164–0281–7

Acknowledgments

THE AUTHORS wish to express their debt of gratitude to pre-
viously published works on Father Paul of Graymoor. These
include *Father Paul: Apostle of Unity*, by Father Titus Cranny,
S.A., (Graymoor Press, Peekskill, N.Y., 1965); *Father Paul and
Christian Unity*, by Father Titus Cranny, S.A., (Chair of Unity
Apostolate, Graymoor, Garrison, N.Y., 1963); *A Woman of
Unity*, by Sister Mary Celine, S.A., (Franciscan Sisters of the
Atonement, Graymoor, Garrison, N.Y., 1956); and *Father
Paul of Graymoor*, by Father David Gannon, S.A., (Macmillan
Company, New York, 1951). From this last work the authors
have taken, in a slightly modified version, the chapter in this
present work, entitled "Life With Father Paul," in the belief

that they could not adequately imitate the personal recollections of Father Gannon, who lived with the founder for many
years.

Special acknowledgment is given to Father Michael Sugrue,
S.A., a close associate and assistant of Father Paul's, who
read the manuscript of this present work, offered many help-
ful suggestions, and whose extensive research on the founder
was of invaluable aid.

A special thank you to our faithful and patient secretary,
Justine Vespermann, is less than adequate.

To the members of our Atonement community whose
encouragement was a constant inspiration, we express our
sincere thanks.

Contents

Introduction

The authors of *Prophet of Reunion* have the courage to state the historic Anglican-Roman Catholic issues in a day when it is the style to minimize the differences and pretend that they do not count.

The long agonizing journey of the Rev. Lewis Wattson, one time Rector of St. John's Church, Kingston, in the Episcopal Diocese of New York, to become the Rev. Paul James Francis Wattson, S.A., is spelled out here in detail. The tensions that developed between Wattson and his fellow Episcopal priests; the agony Wattson went through as he tried to be faithful to the vision he was given to establish a religious order dedicated to restoration of the Anglican Communion within the fold of the Roman Church; the humility he needed in order to tolerate the strictures put upon him after he had made the move (e.g., rebaptism for most of the members of the community; Wattson downgraded to the place of a layman while he received his training at St. Joseph's Seminary in Yonkers, New York), all of these are discussed in sensitive detail.

We live in a day when very active discussions are taking place not only between the Church of Rome and the Anglican Communion but also between the Church of Rome and other Christian bodies, such as the Lutherans. With the Anglicans, officially appointed groups are meeting at the international level (ARCIC), at the national level as in the U.S.A. (A.R.C.), and at the area level as has been the case in New York and in many other cities.

These New York discussions have already produced very interesting results. In 1971 we worked together to arrange simultaneous joint clergy conferences in eighteen local areas of our common geographical responsibility, and into each conference we beamed a closed circuit T.V. broadcast emanating from the facility at St. Joseph's Seminary.

The moderator of that program was the late Bishop Bayne, former Executive Officer of the Anglican Communion, and at that time at the General Theological Seminary. Major statements were made by the Rev. Herbert Ryan, S.J., at that time on the faculty of Woodstock College, and the Rev. Robert Terwilliger, Director of Trinity Institute. The program was introduced by taped statements by Terence Cardinal Cooke and the Rt. Rev. Horace W.B. Donegan. After an hour of statements and discussion the telecast closed down so each local group could discuss and raise questions which were transmitted by telephone to the T.V. station. At the end of the forty-five minutes of discussion the telecast opened up again to deal with the questions that had been raised. The original group was joined by the Monsignor James Rigney, Chairman of the Ecumenical Commission for the Archdiocese, and myself as Chairman of the Episcopal Eumenical Commission. Not all of the questions that had been telephoned in could be answered in the half-hour telecast that followed. The next year we used the same format for conferences for the laity.

Such projects would not have been possible twenty years ago and certainly there were few discussions at any level in Lewis Wattson's day. The recent publications on Eucharist and on Ministry, developed by the International ARC Group, and announced by both His Holiness, Pope Paul, and Michael, Archbishop of Canterbury, are startling evidence of what can happen now.

Undoubtedly, the prophetic ministry of Father Paul of Graymoor and the Society of the Atonement he founded were forerunners of the present openness between the two churches. Whatever suffering was endured in this quest may well have been worth the agony.

In this decade Graymoor stands as a great center of Christian hospitality for groups and individuals. There moves in the midst of the community a fascinating joy of life. It is this freedom and acceptance that makes me feel at home among them, and on each of my visits I cast myself verbally in the role of a building inspector, there to check up on what care they are taking of "our real estate!" I report it amazingly improved since Father Paul took it with him when he and the struggling little community "went to Rome."

November 20, 1974   *J. Stuart Wetmore*
                              Suffragan Bishop of New York

Prophet of Reunion

I

Preaching Such Popery

IN 1901 A YOUNG EPISCOPAL PRIEST, who believed in Christian unity but who lived in a world which was jealously divided, was forced by circumstance and his own convictions out onto that lonely promontory where only prophets, or perhaps fools, dare to tread. The scene was the familiar American arena for intellectual conflict, before a congregation in a pulpit. The young priest was known for his eloquence and his high church and Roman sympathies. The congregation was large, expectant—and low church. The young man had been warned to put civility before conviction. At the last minute, after the agony of decision that haunts the religiously committed, he spoke his mind and was hooted from the pulpit. But what he could not bring together in the world, he brought together in himself. Thus began his movement from the Episcopal Church to the Roman Catholic Church, a movement characterized by acceptance not rejection, by incorporation not exclusion. At a time when it seemed impossible, he maintained both the validity of Anglican orders and the primacy of the pope. His struggle tells us something about the way the Churches are inexorably drawn in behind the emergence of an idea whose time has come again. He was Lewis Wattson, later known as the Reverend Paul James Francis Wattson, S.A., founder of the Society of the Atonement and an advocate of Christian unity.

Wattson had a college friend, the Reverend Charles A. Jessup, who was the rector of Holy Trinity Church at Greenport, Long Island. As time drew near for a meeting of the Archdeaconry of Long Island on September 10th, 1901, Jessup invited his friend, who was known as a forceful preacher, to give the principal sermon. It was friendship rather than an alignment of ideological views that prompted the invitation, since Father Wattson was well known for his eccentric belief that the Anglican Church as a whole should re-establish its pre-Reformation ties with the Church of Rome. Such a position was hardly popular in the American Episcopal Church at the time.

As the time for the meeting drew near, Father Wattson wrote his friend announcing the topic of his sermon: "The Reunion of Christendom and the Chair of Peter." Jessup panicked, called the Archdeacon of Long Island, and together they found a way to forestall the pro-Roman sermon. On the day of the meeting an unsuspecting Father

Wattson boarded the train for Long Island, expecting to be met by his friend Charles Jessup. About halfway to his destination, the archdeacon got on the train and, after a cordial greeting, said to Wattson, "By the by, I hope you do not intend preaching anything very high church tonight. The people of Greenport are decidedly low church and it would be very unfortunate if the sermon gave offense to anyone." Wattson said nothing, but when they got to the station the archdeacon admonished him to "preach them a spiritual sermon."

That evening the attending clergy gathered in the church for Evensong according to the Book of Common Prayer. A fiery North of Ireland clergyman, well-known for his anti-Catholic bias, read the Lesson from the second chapter of Ezechiel: "Son of man, stand upon thy feet, and I will speak unto thee . . . . whether they will hear, or whether they will forbear (for they are a rebellious house), yet shall they know that there has been a prophet among them. And thou, son of man, be not afraid of them, neither be afraid of their words, though briars and thorns be with thee."

That settled it for Wattson. He knelt in silence during the singing of the hymn before the sermon, praying for the strength of Ezechiel, and mounted the steps to the pulpit.

He said he had been asked to speak on the spirit of the missions and would base his sermon on the story in the Acts of the Apostles about Peter and John finding a lame man begging alms at the Beautiful Gate of the Temple in Jerusalem. Lewis Wattson's melodic yet vibrant voice carried Peter's response to the request for alms to the furthermost corners of the church. "Silver and gold have I none, but such as I have I give unto thee; in the name of Jesus Christ of Nazareth rise up and walk." As Scripture tells us, Peter took his hand, pulled him to his feet, and the cured man leapt up and went into the Temple with them, dancing and shouting the praises of God.

He went on to say that when one compared the task of evangelizing the world entrusted by Christ to his followers with the fact that most of mankind was still unconverted, when the vigor of the contemporary Church in its missionary efforts was so lamentable compared with the flaming zeal of the Church as shown forth in the Acts of the Apostles, any sincere Christian could not help but ask the cause of this unhappy situation. Why this annual begging of alms for bankrupt missionary boards, and why so few conversions to show for the sums already spent, Father Wattson asked?

The answer he arrived at was the same as the conclusion reached some years later by the Edinburgh Missionary Conference of 1910. How could the world believe the Gospel if the followers of Christ were divided into Roman Catholic, Orthodox, Anglican, and Protestant splinters? Was not Christian unity the prerequisite of missionary effectiveness? "That they all may be one . . . that the world may believe that thou hast sent me." So Jesus prayed in the 17th chapter of St. John's Gospel. It was this conviction at Edinburgh that evangelism was impossible without ecumenism, which gave birth to what we now know as the Ecumenical Movement. But Lewis Wattson went further.

In the lame man of the Temple he found a figure and type of the Anglican Church (and of every Church, he might have added), desperately needing a miracle. Who gave him that miracle but St. Peter, the Vicar of Jesus Christ and visible head of the Church on earth? How could this necessary reconstitution of the strength and unity Christ willed for his followers take place other than around Christ's vicar, the Pope of Rome? "If we but fix our eye on Him," Father Wattson told his Anglican hearers, "and ask the favor of *corporate admission* into the temple of Christian Unity, from which Henry and Elizabeth Tudor expelled the English people, the Anglo-Saxon race would become the mightiest missionary power in Christendom." Like the great English missionaries of yore, Wilfred, Willibrod, and Boniface, English and American missionaries could convert the world if "once again they took their marching orders from the Vicar of Christ."

Pandemonium broke out in the church, and the North of Ireland presbyter who had unwittingly strengthened Wattson's courage with his thunderous reading from Ezechiel, rushed to the archdeacon and, in a rasping stage whisper, exclaimed, "You cannot allow that man to go on preaching such popery: *you must stop him!*"

Things had clearly gotten out of hand, and the poor archdeacon, who had been crippled some years before in a railroad accident, limped up the altar steps with the help of his cane, graphically illustrating in his own infirmity the thesis of the outrageous sermon. He effectively silenced Father Wattson by shouting out an offertory verse, the signal for the ushers to take the collection: "Let your light so shine before men that they may see your good works and glorify your Father which is in heaven."

The reaction of his friends can be imagined. A woman stopped him the next morning, looked him in the eye and said "Oh, Lewis, how could you?" before walking away. The irate Irishman loudly demanded his ecclesiastical censure at the archdeaconry meeting. There were less than subtle suggestions that the Protestant Episcopal Church in the United States could do without the service of this papal partisan.

Another clergyman, also an Irishman, came to his defense however. "We of the archdeaconry," he said, "have invited a brother clergyman of another diocese, in good canonical standing, to preach before us; and forthwith we proceed to indict the preacher as a heretic without the semblance of an ecclesiastical trial, and bring him before the Church at large as a *traitor*; and all because he has advocated reunion with the Mother Church of Rome, from which we were separated in an evil hour." The threat of censure was dropped, but Father Wattson subsequently found Anglican pulpits closed to him.

Thirty-nine years later, in the last month of his life, Father Wattson recounted this story in a sermon, one of his last. He loved to tell this incident which, viewed over the span of years, was so rich in meaning and pregnant with humor. He always claimed he had the last word because, as the ushers thundered down the aisle and caught him in mid-sentence, his last words were "The Chair of Peter." They were among his last in any Anglican pulpit.

Even in our day of ecumenical tolerance such a sermon would disturb many, but three-quarters of a century ago it was simply outrageous. What accounted for these bizarre views of Christian unity and pro-Romanism expressed within the Episcopal Church?

From its parent body, the Church of England, the American Episcopal Church inherited both Catholic and Protestant traditions. England had been relatively faithful (with some notable exceptions) in its loyalty to Rome before the Reformation in the 16th century. The national

Church established by the Tudors was considered to be a purified continuation of the medieval establishment rather than a clear break with the past. Anglicans could and did emphasize either the pre-Reformation Catholic elements of their heritage or the post-Reformation Protestant traditions while still remaining in the one national English Church. The former came to be known as the "high church" or Anglo-Catholic wing of Anglicanism in the 19th century, while those of Protestant orientation were called the "low church" or evangelical party. Both existed in England and America within one Church, and Anglicans thought of themselves as a bridge between Rome and the Reformers, incorporating the best of many traditions into their Church life.

To understand Lewis Wattson and his sermon, one must go back to the origins of Anglo-Catholicism in the 19th century. In 1833 John Keble preached a sermon at Oxford which is generally considered as the beginning of an effort on the part of many in the Church of England to re-emphasize the positive aspects of pre-Reformation ecclesiastical life lost in the Reformation. His ideas were widely disseminated in the series of pamphlets called *Tracts for the Times*, and he was soon joined by Hurrell Froude, Edward Bouverie Pusey, and John Henry Newman. Collectively they addressed themselves to a search for the causes of the decline in the vitality of the Church of England in their day. Most adherents of the movement demanded the return to the Catholic traditions of the Church, which they defined in the terms of St. Vincent of Lerins as that which had been believed "everywhere, always and by all," and interpreted in the practical order as referring to the generally received tradition of the Christian Church before the division of East and West in the 11th century. This general tradition they held to have been defined by the first seven ecumenical councils of the undivided Church. The legitimate heirs of that Church, they thought, were the three great communions, Eastern Orthodox, Roman Catholic, and Anglican, together with some minor groups which had maintained the succession of bishops without interruption and remained substantially orthodox in doctrine. These religious bodies together constituted the one Catholic Church.

The Oxford Movement met violent opposition from Protestant elements in the Church of England, especially when it attempted to celebrate the liturgy of the Church in a manner which seemed to be an imitation of contemporary Roman Catholic usage. Although they claimed to be simply emphasizing their Catholic heritage, the Oxfordians were constantly accused of being subversive Romanizers, and their position within the Church of England was further exacerbated by the secession of Newman and many of his followers to Roman Catholicism in the 1840s and thereafter.

By 1843 the controversy reached America, where New York City's General Theological Seminary became a center of the movement. As in England, some Anglicans became Roman Catholics. Some who remained entirely faithful were subjected to ecclesiastical scrutiny, and as the hunt for subversives gained momentum, rectors of parishes and bishops of dioceses were brought to trial. But the high-church movement continued to spread, reviving an increasing number of medieval customs, imitating those of current Roman Catholicism, and emphasizing doctrinal positions in contradistinction to the Protestant heritage of the Church.

Religious brotherhoods and sisterhoods were reintroduced for the first time since the Reformation, and some even attempted unsuccessfully to change the name of the Church from "Protestant Episcopal" to "American Catholic."

Interest in the reunion of Christendom was always high in the Anglican communion both in England and America, possibly because of the ability to look in both Catholic and Protestant directions and to maintain some contact with both traditions. Episcopal ecumenism, however, rarely included the pope. In 1865 a resolution was passed expressing sympathy with the efforts of those within the "Italian Church" to bring about a Reformation, and the House of Deputies, which, with the House of Bishops, constitutes the Church's governing body, announced "that all those branches of the Apostolic Church which accept the Holy Scriptures and the Niceo-Constantino-politan Creed, and which reject the usurpations and innovations of the Bishop of Rome are called . . . to renew those primitive relations which the Roman schism has interrupted."

Perhaps a more positive ecumenical contribution was the so-called Chicago Quadrilateral or fourfold platform put forth as the basis of proposals for unity by the Anglican communion which included the Holy Scriptures as the Word of God, the Apostles' and Nicene Creeds as the rule of faith, the two sacraments of baptism and Holy Communion, and the episcopate as the keystone of governmental unity. The Quadrilateral was accepted in a declaration by the House of Bishops in 1886 and reaffirmed by the international gathering of the national Anglican churches at Lambeth, England, the next year.

Like most high churchmen before him, Lewis Wattson

faced the cruel dilemma, so graphically depicted in his Long Island sermon, of either remaining within the Anglican communion, thus suffering separation from the pre-Reformation center of his Church, the Bishop of Rome, or leaving the Church he loved in order to seek reconciliation with the papacy. What made his position unique was that he insisted on espousing both the corporate reunion of the Anglican Church, whose ministry and sacraments he regarded as valid, with the See of Rome, and the doctrine of papal primacy and infallibility as defined by the First Vatican Council of 1870. Two years after the sermon he wrote: "We believe all that the Catholic Episcopate in communion with the Apostolic See of Rome believes, the dogmas of the Immaculate Conception and Papal Infallibility not excepted. But we also believe in Anglican Orders and the perpetuity of the Anglican Church."

Not only did Wattson have difficulty with Anglicans who rejected papal infallibility, but in 1896 Pope Leo XIII in his bull, *Apostolicae Curae*, condemned Anglican orders as "absolutely null and utterly void," and that seemed to be a final rejection by Rome of what Father Wattson would call the perpetuity of the Anglican Church based on two major objections.

Roman Catholic controversialists raised doubts about the actual historical continuity of ordination by the laying on of hands. Some contended, for example, that Anglican Archbishop Parker at the time of the Reformation was not himself validly consecrated or that his principal consecrator, Barlow, had not been consecrated. These historical arguments rested on the assumption that both the physical laying on of hands and a specified interpretation of the rite were essential to the validity of orders. Anglicans countered that even if this succession had been broken by

Parker, it had certainly been restored in subsequent years by bishops consecrated in one of several undisputed non-English successions.

The other line of Roman attack questioned the rite of ordination introduced under King Edward VI because there were no words or acts explicitly conferring the power of priests to offer sacrifice. The Roman Catholic view on Anglican orders was that they were absolutely null and utterly void because of lack of historical continuity, lack of a proper ordination rite, and lack of the intention to ordain priests for the eucharistic sacrifice.

In an encyclical letter of March 29, 1897, the Archbishops of Canterbury and York formulated the Anglican reply which in large part has come to be the view of many contemporary Roman Catholic theologians as well. They contended that all of the ordinals and public acts of the Anglican Church make it clear that she intends to confer the office instituted by Christ and all that it contains, and that the Anglican texts were at least as explicit in regard to the eucharistic sacrifice as the canon of the Roman mass. They pointed out that explicit references required by Leo XIII were not contained in the earliest Roman ordinals, so that if Anglican orders are invalid on this basis, so are those of Rome.

Thus not only did Father Wattson's own Church indignantly reject his notions of papal infallibility, but the very bishop whose claims he championed and into whose jurisdiction he aspired to lead his fellow churchmen had pronounced his own priesthood as "absolutely null and utterly void." That the man should go on insisting that his orders were valid, his Church perpetual, and the Pope who condemned him infallible was a testimony both to a spirit of personal immolation, indefatigable zeal for principle no matter how difficult, and tremendous courage. It was also a very effective way to ruin an ecclesiastical career. Father Wattson was a dead duck in the Episcopal Church of 1901, and if the pope ever heard of him, he was "Mr. Wattson."

How then can one explain that today, less than 40 years after his death in 1940, bishops and theologians representing both the worldwide Anglican communion and the Roman Catholic Church could issue a bilateral statement announcing their substantive agreement on the nature of Holy Orders with the recommendation that their two Churches recognize each other's ministries and sacraments and proceed step by step to intercommunion? And who would have expected that Pope Paul VI would refer to the Anglican communion as "our Sister Church?" Who, listening to that Long Island sermon, would have believed that another inter-Church dialogue in the 1970s would suggest that a renewed papacy would be no obstacle to Christian reunion?

What is evident is that the progression of theological thought in both Churches has gone far beyond the narrow confines of 19th-century polemics. Victorian Roman Catholics and Anglicans were out to prove each other wrong. Their contemporary descendents have rallied to the standard of Pope John XXIII: "I stand for what unites and I hold at a distance those things which divide."

What seemed irreconcilable and preposterous in 1901— belief in Anglican orders and belief in Roman primacy—is no longer absurd. What is significant about Father Wattson is that in his own person he was a precursor of that ecumenical development which, in the course of time, would bring the Anglican and Roman communions within sight of reconciliation.

II
A Jesuit in Disguise

GENERAL THEOLOGICAL SEMINARY in New York, was in a state of angry ferment in the 1840s. John Henry Newman's *Tract 90*, which had been recently published in England, contended that the *Thirty-nine Articles of Religion* contained in the Anglican Book of Common Prayer could somehow be reconciled by an ingenious theological interpretation with the decrees of the Council of Trent, Roman Catholicism's militant counterattack on the religious revolt of the 16th century. Copies of the tract were clandestinely circulated among students and faculty at the seminary, and there was talk of dreadful Romanish plots to subvert the Protestant character of the Episcopal Church.

Into this pressure cooker of heady controversy in 1843 walked Joseph Newton Wattson, Lewis Wattson's father, raised a Presbyterian and now preparing for the priesthood in the Episcopal Church.

Joseph Wattson came from the so-called border states of Delaware and Maryland, that area in pre-Civil War America schizophrenically situated between the North and the South. His politics, like his religion, trod a thin line between warring camps. He was a southern sympathizer living in the North, a Presbyterian who became a high church Anglican. A man of stubborn courage, ready wit, and facile tongue, he was once threatened by a Yankee lynch mob and talked his way out.

One day, as Lewis Wattson recalled the story in later years, several students gathered in Joseph Wattson's room at the seminary for a bull session. The topic as usual was the controversial *Tracts*. A rumor had been circulating in the seminary that there were a couple of Jesuit spies enrolled whose sinister task it was to indoctrinate a chosen cabal of students so that upon ordination they could lead their congregations into Roman allegiance. A seminarian named Prescott, a somewhat humorless and gullible person, knocked at Joseph Wattson's door, looked cautiously in, and in a stage whisper said to Wattson, "Have you heard the rumor?"

"What rumor?"

"Why the one about the Jesuit spies."

In an ill-considered moment of flippancy, Joseph replied, "Why Prescott, didn't you know that?"

Prescott repeated the remark to the dean, and the authorities panicked. Wattson and a roommate of his, Donnelly, whose Irish name aroused suspicion despite the fact that he personally was an evangelical, were both expelled in 1844.

The two "Jesuits" now found themselves out on the street. As they were walking around lower New York in a state of shock, they happened to come upon the old St. Patrick's Cathedral on Mulberry Street, the seat of New York's Roman Catholic Bishop Hughes, himself a fiery figure who once threatened to burn down a Protestant church for every Catholic edifice destroyed by the Know-Nothings. "Wattson, the Episcopal Church has behaved toward us like a stepmother," Donnelly snorted in a pique of temper. "Let's go round the corner and call on Bishop Hughes." The more level-headed Wattson replied, "Let's sleep over the matter first."

The Jesuit incident followed both seminarians to their grave. Donnelly was eventually admitted to the Episcopal ministry and for a while was an assistant to the influential Dr. Seabury, editor of the *Churchman*, but the Jesuit label stuck and his career was ruined. The last years of his life were spent in a lonely West Virginia mission where he died in poverty and obscurity.

Joseph Wattson, like his friend, persisted in being ordained in a Church which never trusted him. Years afterwards, after a dreary succession of poor parishes, he narrowly missed appointment as the rector of a plum parish in Baltimore when the vestry was tipped off about his expulsion from the seminary. Finding a bishop for his ordination was also a difficulty. He first approached Bishop Lee of Delaware, an evangelical, who dismissed him with the tart remark, "Young man, go to Rome, for that is where you belong!" Finally, the more Catholic-minded Bishop Whittingham of Maryland, who had himself suffered evangelical opposition in his diocese, ordained Wattson. After a number of difficult assignments in wretchedly poor parishes, he was at last offered the rectorship of St. Clement's at Massey, Kent County, Maryland. Here Wattson found the only security and permanency he had ever known in his ministry and he remained for 25 years as rector.

Civil war was raging in the United States when a third son was born to Joseph Wattson on July 16th, 1863. His wife, Mary Electa, had been twice widowed before marrying the rector, and at this baby's birth she despaired at providing for another mouth. Their son was born during the difficult and impoverished war-time days and, in hope of an inheritance, was named Lewis after a rich railroad tycoon relative. They added Thomas as a middle name after the apostle whose doubts gave way to firm faith.

Lewis Thomas Wattson was a quiet, ordinary boy, and a strong bond of affection united the now elderly Joseph Wattson with his youngest son. The father was a great storyteller and would entertain Lewis by the hour with his stories, the favorite always being "The Jesuits in Disguise." The rector could tell it humorously now, devoid of all bitterness despite his sufferings. One day after returning from a parish sick call, Joseph Wattson and his son Lewis were sitting in the study of the rectory awaiting the dinner hour. The boy was about ten years old, but even at that age he was clearly interested in religion as the father talked about his Church, her teachings and her ritual. He talked about some of his old seminary friends and what had happened to them. Some, like himself, had remained high church Anglicans, while others had become Roman Catholics. "Once I was present," the father told Lewis, "in the Roman Catholic cathedral of Baltimore, when Walworth, as a Paulist

Father, addressed a vast concourse of men who packed the building to the doors. You see, Walworth and I were students together at the 'General'. . . . What we need in the Episcopal Church is a preaching order like the Paulists."

In the last year of his life Lewis wrote, "Although at the time I had never seen a Catholic priest in all my life and knew nothing about the religious life which flourishes in the Catholic Church, an interior Voice said to my intelligence, 'That is what you will do some day, found a preaching order like the Paulists.' Now was that just a figment of imagination on my part or was it the Voice of the Holy Spirit, intimating to me the plans God had for my future? I will have to leave the answer to that question to yourself."

Lewis received his early education in a little rural school close to his father's rectory, and then his secondary education at St. Mary's Hall, a private church school in Burlington, New Jersey. He next entered St. Stephen's College at Annandale, New York, where a friend later remembered him as somewhat serious, in the top tenth of his class, a good tennis player, and though devout, not ostentatiously religious. This friend would later become Father Paul's hapless host at the infamous Long Island sermon.

Money for Wattson at college was always a problem. During one school recess he tried selling patented ironing boards from a buckboard. Unfortunately, on entering a town to begin his sales he ran over a chicken. Searching out the owner, he offered a free ironing board in compensation, and that was the only "sale" he made that day. He somehow lacked the courage to ask strangers for their patronage. He would talk about everything but ironing boards to prospective customers, and once was pleasantly

surprised when a farmer bought one without being solic-
ited. Eventually, Lewis's stepsister took over the business in
order to insure his expenses at school.

In the fall of 1882 Lewis Wattson enrolled at his
father's alma mater, General Theological Seminary in New
York. In later years he told of a strange feeling that came
over him as he entered its portals. "I thought that being the
son of a man who had been asked to leave because of his
'Romanish leanings,' I would always be under surveillance."
After 20 years, however, the story about the Jesuits in disguise had been forgotten. But he took no chances. Charles
Jessup, his roommate for eight years in college and in the
seminary, remarked: "We never spoke on the subject of
reunion."

Friends described him during this period as short in
stature, with light hair and delicate features, a sparkling eye
and a sense of humor, an original, independent figure who
articulated his ideas forcefully.

Lewis's ordination to the diaconate in 1885 took place
in Maryland, where illness prevented Bishop Henry C. Lay
of Easton from presiding. He delegated Bishop Alfred Lee
of Delaware to act in his place, the same Lee who 40 years
earlier had refused to ordain the father because of his suspi-
cious Catholic associations. At the dinner following the
ceremony, the bishop, with tears in his eyes, admitted his
error of years ago and expressed regret at his behavior.
Perhaps Joseph saw in his son the vindication of his own
years of suffering, and Lewis looked up to his father not
only as a parent but as the model of the churchman he himself wanted to be.

There was a shortage of clergy at the time in the Episcopal Church, so immediately upon ordination to the dia-

conate, Lewis Wattson was given the care of St. James's Church in Port Deposit, Maryland, even though he could not officiate at the Communion service. His father performed this function for him, and when an invitation came to the elder Wattson to become rector of St. John's Episcopal Church at Kingston, New York, five months later, he suggested that since he had already retired, his son, an excellent preacher, should be called in his place. This was agreed to, and Lewis became one of the youngest rectors in the history of the Episcopal Church. In 1885 he moved with his parents to Kingston where he stayed for ten years.

Lewis Wattson was ordained as a priest the following year at the age of 23 by a special dispensation, since the canons of the Episcopal Church required the candidates for the ministry to be 24 years of age. When his father died in 1887, the full duties of the parish fell to the son. "I can see him now," one of his parishioners of those days said. "He would preach in his parish church, his wonderful voice touching all our hearts, his teaching appealing to us and making us better churchmen and churchwomen. He had a habit (probably you noticed it) while preaching, of grasping a black cross which hung around his neck, as much as to say, 'In the Cross of Christ I glory!' "

In May 1894 he began the publication of *The Pulpit of the Cross*, which was originally intended to be simply a parish bulletin, but his outspoken Catholic views soon gained him a far wider audience. "Our policy will be aggressive rather than defensive," he wrote in the first issue. His early articles were entitled "The Doctrine of the Real Presence," "Extreme Unction," "The Forgiveness of Sins," "The Sacrifice of the Mass." In one edition he wrote: "Evidently it was in the mind of the Divine Author of the

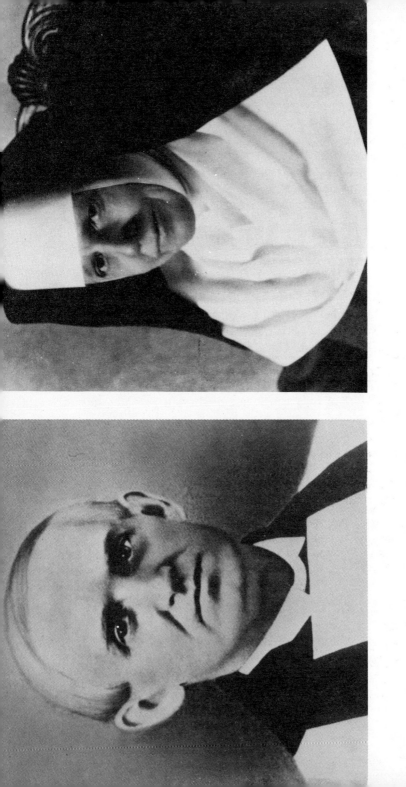

Joseph Wattson and Mother Lurana

Christian religion to found on earth not many Protestant sects but one universal Church, and both the Old and New Testaments tell us the same thing." He taught the branch theory of high Anglicanism, which held that the Church was composed of three main branches—Roman, Greek, and Anglican. "But what do you understand this one true Church of Divine Authority to be?" one reader inquired. "I understand that it is to be that mighty Christian organism which has come down to us from Jesus and his apostles under the name of the Holy Catholic Church and which exists today in three great historic communions: Roman, Greek, and Anglican communions, which last comprises all the English-speaking Christians throughout the world who are members of the Anglo-Catholic Church." He went further, and in July 1895 he wrote in his editorial:

The Roman Church bases her claim to spiritual jurisdiction over the United States, along with the whole world besides, upon the doctrine of Papal Supremacy, which doctrine is that the Bishop of Rome is the Vicar of Jesus Christ on earth, the supreme ruler and head of the Catholic Church, and that it is necessary to salvation, for every human being, to acknowledge the Pope's authority and believe in his infallibility. Either the doctrine is true or it is false; if it is true, there is no Catholic Church apart from the Pope, nor indeed any Christianity. If it be false, every other argument which the Church of Rome might put forth in defence of her position is vitiated and made of no effect by this one gigantic error. . . . We appeal to history. . . . The argument from history as well as from Scripture is fatal to the Papal theories of the Church of Rome, and we cannot regard the Roman Catholic hierarchy in America in any other light than being the representatives of a foreign bishop, having no lawful jurisdiction in the United States.

Wattson's Anglican background allowed him to give

no place as yet for Roman intrusions into his Anglo-Saxon world. Apparently his reputation carried far and wide, because *The New York Sun* remarked that he would become a Catholic in the not-too-distant future. Father Wattson indignantly replied: "We were baptized into the Holy Catholic Church over thirty years ago, and please God, we expect to continue a Catholic until we die."

These were busy years for Father Wattson. He built a mission church, named for the Holy Cross as the work of the parish expanded. He is remembered for his many works of charity. Once a poor man and his wife were stranded in town and could not get out to their distant farm. They came to the rectory seeking aid and Father Wattson put them in the guest room, fed them, and gave them some money the next morning. When his mother ("short, stout, and snappy" according to a neighbor), who served as his housekeeper, returned, she was quite incensed. "What? In the guest bed, with my guest sheets on it, and you don't even know who they are?"

Wattson was a man of prayer. One night the sexton came to see if the church had been locked up, and as he lit the gas jet he heard a cough at the altar. It was one A.M. and Father Wattson was there, praying for the sick of the parish. And always his preaching was remembered. As one parishioner recalled: "When he preached in the little Holy Cross Church he wore a black robe, white covering over it, with long sleeves. He'd lay one arm over the other and preach softly, with no gestures, but you could hear a pin drop. He would not read from the Bible, he knew it."

Amid all his concerns as a busy rector, Father Wattson kept returning in his own mind to that childhood inspiration "You will found a preaching order." It was now

linked up in his mind with the propagation of the Catholic
views he so longed the Episcopal Church to embrace as a
whole. He had resolved his institute would have a name
associated with Christ's atoning sacrifice on Calvary, but all
appropriate ones had already been taken by other Anglican
or Roman Catholic religious orders. One day in his reading
he happened upon a reference to St. Francis by an Anglican
writer, Canon Ferrer, who said that St. Francis was the
most perfect imitator of Jesus Christ. Pulling down an
encyclopedia, Wattson read the entry on St. Francis.
There he read the story of how the young Francis, like
Wattson, thought of beginning life as a religious. Being in
doubt, he went to a church and asked a priest in the name
of the Holy Trinity to open the Scripture. Then Francis
put his finger on the book without looking, opened his eyes
and read the text as an answer from God regarding his own
problem. Each time he did this, Francis noticed that the
text applied to leaving all and following Christ.

"Why cannot God guide his servant the same as he
guided St. Francis?" Father Wattson asked himself. Why
couldn't God himself give a name to the new institute that
he believed he was called upon to found? In 1893, just 60
years after John Keble preached his famous sermon on
national apostasy at St. Mary's, Oxford, Father Wattson
resolved to find God's will by literally imitating St. Francis
of Assisi.

"Impressed with this thought, namely, that God would
give a name for this institute, on the seventh Sunday after
Pentecost, July 9th, 1893, after Communion Service, I took
down the Bible from which it was customary for me to
read my Scripture section before preaching. The congregation had gone from the church and I was alone. Kneeling

at the foot of the altar, I laid the book on the top step, invoked the Blessed Trinity, opened the book without looking, put my finger on the opening page . . . I discovered our first text from St. John VII: 37-39."

In the last day, that great day of the Feast, Jesus stood and cried, saying, "If any man thirst, let him come unto me, and drink. He that believeth on me, as the scripture hath said, out of his belly shall flow rivers of living water." (But this spake he of the Spirit, which they that believe on Him should receive: for the Holy Ghost was not yet given: because that Jesus was not yet glorified.)

Initially disappointed that the text did not refer to the idea of atonement, Father Wattson on further reflection sought in this text the promise of the Holy Spirit for the preaching order he was going to found. He opened the book a second time and his finger fell upon Romans V:11, "And not only so, but we also joy in God, through our Lord Jesus Christ, by whom we have now received the atonement."

Some years later he wrote, "The moment my eyes rested upon the word 'Atonement' it seemed to stand out from that sacred page with the distinctness all its own and it flashed upon me, as I believe from Heaven, that the community God was preparing was to be called the Society of the Atonement."

From his early childhood Lewis had been fascinated by the Cross. As a little boy he fashioned one himself out of two sticks, and fastened it upon the wall of his bedroom. Before it he performed his morning and evening devotions. It was his devotion to the Cross which made him insist that the name of the preaching institute of his childhood dreams be associated with the central act of the redemption. Now he had a name—Society of the Atonement—given, he believed, by God himself.

At the third opening of the book, he came upon St. Paul's description of the institution of the Holy Eucharist in the 11th chapter of I Corinthians. Thus, from the hand of God himself came the name of the society and its spiritual constitution. First there was to be the quickening, inspiring power of the Holy Spirit; then the crowning act of redeeming love, the atonement of Christ upon the Cross; and lastly the sacrifice of the Mass, by means of which the atonement of Christ is perpetuated.

"I went over to the rectory immediately and wrote down the texts," he reported later. Then, for the second time in my life, I was warned by the same interior Voice I had heard as a boy: 'You will have to wait seven years for this to be realized.' So I laid the paper aside and went on with my work as though nothing had happened."

He had his name, derived from the King James version of Romans V: 11. It was associated with the Cross, but what did it have to do with his vision of Christian unity, the reconciliation of the Anglican Church with Rome? In modern versions of the Bible the word "atonement" is translated as "reconciliation," because the original meaning of the word "atonement" was "at-one-ment." To make at one, to reconcile all men with God, was the fruit of Christ's redeeming sacrifice at Calvary. Gradually the English word "atonement," the only original contribution of the English language to the theological lexicon, shifted in its meaning from the effect of Christ's sacrifice, reconciliation, to the means by which it was attained, satisfaction for the sins of mankind. In common English parlance, at-one-ment meaning reconciliation became atonement signifying satisfaction. But Father Wattson was primarily inspired and motivated by the name "atonement" in the context of Romans V: 11—as reconciliation.

His mission was to reconcile the Anglican and Roman Churches, and he explained this as follows:

It is recorded that in a vision to Edward the Confessor, the Church of England was cut off as a tree and carried three furlongs distance, then by no human power, brought back and set on its stock again. No act is similar to that in history except the act of Henry VIII who, in 1533, finally separated the Church of England from its allegiance to the Holy See. If three furlongs be taken as a span of time—that is, three centuries—it brings us to the year 1833, the year the Oxford Movement began and produced John *Henry* Newman, the Newman or the *new Henry*. John Henry Newman gave to the movement what he declared as its terminus *ad quem*, union with Rome. Continuing this line of thought, it was the seventh Sunday after Pentecost that Keble's sermon began the Oxford Movement in 1833, and it was just sixty years afterwards, on the seventh Sunday after Pentecost, that the Atonement texts were given to the Father Founder.

What was he to do now? He was a great believer in symbolism. He believed the Voice had told him to wait seven years for the accomplishment of his vision. Three times he had invoked the Holy Trinity, three texts were given, three hundred years passed between Henry VIII's break with Rome and Keble's beginning of the Oxford Movement. That famous sermon was given on the seventh Sunday after Pentecost, the same seventh Sunday on which 60 years later he had received the texts, and he must wait seven years for their fulfillment. Throughout his life he saw the hand of God mysteriously indicated in mystical numbers in a manner almost reminiscent of medieval cabalists. And the mystical imagination is one that seeks and apprehends essential unity in diversity and contrarities.

The following two years were spent in routine parochial duties, but a change came in 1895 when a request came from a group of unmarried Episcopal clergymen who were leading a semimonastic life in Omaha, Nebraska, under the spiritual direction of Bishop George Worthington. They called themselves the Associate Mission and had as their aim the evangelization of out-of-the-way places which lacked clergy. They needed a superior, and would Father Wattson consider accepting this position?

The seven years were not up, but could this be part of God's plan in the formation of the Society of the Atonement? He decided to take the chance, and his parishioners seemed to understand although they were sorry to lose him. "Father Wattson was never quite satisfied with parochial life," one of them remembered. "Always he appealed to me as one who was fitted—one might say called—to the monastic life. His was essentially a spiritual nature, and unconsciously we all recognized the fact that his life was on a higher plane than the ordinary churchman."

His mother accompanied him to Omaha where she died two years later. The work there was more satisfying to Father Wattson than any he had ever done. His subjects were all of a common mind, bound together in a common cause. "Mass, Matins and Mush" was the bulk of their daily schedule one member recalled. Mornings were devoted to study, afternoons to missionary journeys. New mission stations were added to the apostolic work of the members, but Father Wattson was more interested in their life at home. Oblivious to increasing opposition of some members, he gradually imposed a more rigid rule of life which included spiritual reading at meals and silence throughout the house. Some members protested they were not Benedictines. In later years he recalled sadly his mistake in trying to make monks out of men who did not want to be monks. He was described by one who knew him then as a rigorist. He kept certain hours of silence; if those in the house who knew his custom spoke, he would not answer unless charity demanded. "Father Paul was not chummy with any of the men in the house; he was a good organizer, but he was extremely busy, and, when not busy, he was occupied with his religious exercises." This friend thought he seemed to be skating on thin ice regarding the Roman question.

Perhaps the future founder of a religious order did not fully realize that the Omaha venture was an *Associate* Mission. Perhaps he was not used to working with other men on the basis of equality. His monastic hankerings and Roman leanings combined into a heady brew too strong for his associates. The Associate Mission was not the foundation of his new institute. He would have to wait the full seven years.

III

The Palace of Lady Poverty

THE QUEST OF LEWIS WATTSON for a basis on which to build his future Society of the Atonement, now named but still without form or substance, took a new turn in 1896. Still in the midst of his work at the Associate Mission in Omaha he received a letter from a sister belonging to a diocesan community for women in Albany, New York. Her name was Lurana Mary White. Unlike Wattson, she came from a wealthy family. From her earliest years she had felt a desire to dedicate her life to serving God through ministry to his poor; at 23 a sermon strengthened her conviction. The preacher had remarked: "There may be before me a young woman or a young man who secretly and half-fearfully is worshipping the ideal of a holy dedicated life, the oblation of herself or himself to God. I adjure you be brave and bring that beautiful thing to the light and acknowledge it before God, to yourself and others." "A very short time after this experience," she later wrote in her memoirs, "I knew that God was speaking to my soul more clearly than ever before. . . . I wished to do and suffer something worthwhile for God and for others."

To serve God in his poor she entered the Sisterhood of the Holy Child at Albany, New York. The bishop would not allow the sisters to make formal vows of religion, but with the consent of her spiritual director she privately made vows of poverty, chastity, and obedience. Still she was not satisfied.

In her first letter to Father Wattson in 1896, she asked, "Do you know of any community of sisters in the Episcopal Church vowed to corporate poverty?" In his reply, Wattson lamented that he knew of no such order, but continued: "Worldliness is indeed the most serious hindrance now standing in the way of the Church's onward and upward progress in America, and a religious order either of men or women that would take our Lord's precepts literally, as did Saint Francis, and refuse to possess any property at all might serve as salt to preserve the lump."

During two years of subsequent correspondence the two exchanged their dreams, hopes, and plans in a general way, but Lewis Wattson did not reveal his hopes for the Society of the Atonement in detail.

Lurana White's spiritual pilgrimage continued, and in 1897 she asked to be released from all obligations to the Sisterhood of the Holy Child and she journeyed to London where she entered the novitiate of the Sisters of Bethany.

Father Wattson had advised her that after her religious training there she would be better prepared to return to America and undertake the foundation of her own sisterhood dedicated to corporate poverty. After completing a year's stay with the Sisters of Bethany, she was clothed in a Franciscan habit and set off on a pilgrimage to Rome and Assisi. At the tomb of St. Francis she prayed for his spirit and help in her project. At St. Peter's in Rome she carefully eluded her Protestant companions by diverting their attention to a side chapel, and once alone, hastily knelt to kiss the bronze foot of the fisherman's statue while making an interior act of allegiance to the Prince of the Apostles and his successor, the reigning Pope Leo XIII.

Upon her return from Europe to her family home, "The Terrace" at Warwick, New York, she wrote to Father Wattson for further advice. It turned out that he too had been involved in an extended and painful re-evaluation of his position.

While Lurana White had been venerating the statue of St. Peter in Rome, Lewis Wattson had been wrestling in Omaha with the question of papal primacy. He studied all the authors, pro and con, that he could find but in his own mind he could find no rest. He plowed through Littledale's *Plain Reasons Against Joining the Church of Rome*, Gore's *Roman Catholic Claims*, Puller's *Primitive Saints and the See of Rome*. He weighed these Anglican authors against such Romans as Gibbon in his *Faith of Our Fathers*, Murphy in *The Chair of Peter* and Allies in *Peter, His Name and Office*. He visited Roman Catholic churches and prayed for light before the flickering sanctuary lamp that indicated the Real Presence of Christ in the Blessed Sacrament.

Father Wattson took his perplexities to his ecclesiastical superior, Bishop Worthington, and to Lurana White. Perhaps he had been mistaken in his hopes of establishing a Society of the Atonement. The project should perhaps be carried out by others who could see their way more clearly. Would Sister Lurana come to Omaha with two other nuns, former companions of hers in the Sisterhood of the Holy Child, in the hope of founding the Sisters of the Atonement He advised his bishop that he felt obliged in conscience to leave his post as superior of the Associate Mission in order to gain time for sorting things out in his own mind. Sister Lurana was appalled at his change of plans. In later years Father Wattson considered this period of indecision on his part to be a temptation of the devil. "Why, the Old Boy almost took the Society of the Atonement away from me in Omaha," he would tell his novices later.

Now he was really alone and at loose ends. On his last day in Omaha in September 1898 he celebrated a private Communion service in the oratory of the mission house. He always remembered his thanksgiving after that service. Up to this time he was more an imitator of St. Paul in his hopes of founding a preaching order than of St. Francis and the ideal of corporate poverty in the service of the poor. It was Lurana White who influenced him in this regard, although the example of St. Francis had played a part in his finding of the name of his society in the years before he met her. Kneeling in prayer he thought of the poor little man of Assisi who, having nothing, yet possessed all things. Father Wattson had nothing—no position, no money, no home. He wasn't even sure if the Episcopal Church was still his spiritual home. If he was to be a preacher, what was he to preach? Where was he to find a pulpit from which to preach? It was the seraphic Poverello—"the little poor one," a name given to St. Francis—who attracted him now, and whose example offered consolation and direction in this bleak moment. With him he would be able to bear all things, believe all things, hope for all things, endure all things.

In his first letter to Lurana White, Father Wattson had indicated his thought that the renunciation of worldly goods could be the lump of yeast to revive the Church infected by worldliness. Now, as he placed himself again at the unqualified disposition of God, he took a vow never to touch money. This was in imitation of St. Francis, who stripped himself naked before his own earthly father in order to follow in complete poverty his Father in Heaven. In literal implementation of what inspired him, Lewis Wattson would be a 20th-century St. Francis. He would depend only on God.

The next morning he got on the train and headed East for the only place he knew to go, his old church in Kingston, New York. In his three-year absence somebody else had taken his place, and he must have arrived in a somewhat self-conscious and depressed state. Now he was back among them not as their rector but as an unemployed clergyman. Where were all his plans now? Had he stayed there, his lot would have been different. Members of the congregation had always been after him to marry and settle down. Indeed, on one occasion during his rectorship, an insistent woman of the congregation had persuaded the gullible Father Wattson that he was obliged to marry her because while driving her home in a buggy during a rainstorm his hand, which was holding up an umbrella, had inadvertently touched the nape of her neck. He was greatly relieved when her subsequent flirtations with others resulted in breaking off the engagement. He told his mother he was never happy about it in the first place.

He had not been satisfied to settle down as a comfortable country rector with a family. He had dreams of bigger things, yet he had nothing to show for it. The Society of the Atonement was still only a name.

At this period of depression, Lurana White invited him to come to her home at Warwick, New York, for a visit. Perhaps they could make a retreat and ask God to show them what to do now. She later recalled in her diary, "Our Father Founder arrived in Warwick toward evening on October 3rd, [1898] the eve of St. Francis Day. On that memorable day we met for the first time. The future Father Founder told the story of his call and his hopes, and I told him of my search for St. Francis and corporate poverty. Then there came to both of us the dawning realization of the oneness of God's call."

Both of them had come to a dead end separately, but now as they shared their dreams the future became suddenly clear. That evening they planned the future Society of the Atonement. They began with three days of prayer in a room set up as a temporary chapel. Sister Lurana wrote, "Then came October 7th and the end of the three days' retreat which we had kept together. Father blessed, and laid on the little improvised altar in the oratory, two crucifixes; one he gave to me and the other he kept for himself. The latter had been brought by me from Assisi, and I had seen it in the Sacro Convento lowered down by the Franciscan Father our guide, until it touched the tomb of St. Francis. It was well understood by the Father Founder, and by me, that these same crucifixes represented the entire oblation of ourselves into the hands of God for the purpose of founding the Society of the Atonement."

Father Wattson left the chapel in high spirits, filled with a sense of security borne on the conviction that God's hand was directing them. He entered his own room, running over in his mind the plans he and Lurana White were making when suddenly and without warning he was plunged into a diabolical despair. What if this whole thing were nothing but a delusion? Who was he to think that Almighty God would entrust to him such an enterprise? How could he mislead Lurana White with false hopes of beginning a religious community? He had no money. Had he forgotten his vow never to touch money?

He was always certain in later years these were nothing but delusions of the devil. Upon his mind there relentlessly pounded the thought, now of satanic rather than divine origin, "You are a fool, that's what you are; you know you have no money; you have no right to take upon yourself the support of that woman. What you should do is leave the Episcopal Church and join the Catholic Church and become a Passionist." One wonders whether the Roman Catholic order of Passionists would have been flattered to receive his application, prompted as he believed, by the devil. It is interesting too that he firmly believed that the temptation to leave the Episcopal Church at this time was a satanic notion.

As he had done so many time before, he sought God's help by opening the Bible at random. He would do anything God wanted if only he would show him the way. When he confidently opened the book his eyes fell upon Chapter VI, Verses 13-18, of St. Paul's Epistle to the

Hebrews. And there the Omnipotent God spoke to him with clarity and forcefulness. Sacred Scripture, in the words of the King James version, once again pointed out the way to Lewis Wattson.

For when God made promise to Abraham, because he could swear by no greater, he sware by himself, saying, "Surely blessing I will bless thee, and multiplying I will multiply thee." And so, after he had patiently endured, he obtained the promise.

For men verily swear by the greater; and an oath for confirmation is to them an end to all strife.

Wherein God, willing more abundantly to shew unto the heirs of promise the immutability of his counsel, confirmed it by an oath; that by two immutable things in which it was impossible for God to lie, we might have a strong consolation, who have fled for refuge to lay hold upon the hope set before us.

With the reading of this passage all doubts about what he should do left Father Wattson. From that day on he and Sister Lurana celebrated October 7th as Covenant Day, and as the years went on he would always read to his community, from the very same Bible he had used on this occasion, the promise of God to his servant. In Abraham he saw himself. He was called upon to leave his own home, his own people, his own country and travel into a promised land that God would show him. His followers would be as numberless as the sands of the seashore and the stars of the sky. Nothing could defeat him now, neither the forces of darkness or the difficulties of this world. He believed he was destined by God to raise up a great religious order like the Benedictines in the Dark Ages, the Franciscans and Dominicans who recalled the Church to its apostolic purity amidst the decadence of the 13th century, the Jesuits who saved the papacy after the challenge of Luther. His Society of the Atonement would be the instrument God would use in the 20th century to bring back all Christians into unity with the See of Peter, and his patron would be St. Francis who had prayed, "Lord make us an instrument of your peace, that where there is hatred we may sow love." After leaving Warwick he wrote to Sister Lurana:

Of all the gracious acts of Divine Providence which have been showered upon me from the day I was born, nothing has been more marvelous or exceedingly precious in my eyes than this wondrous message of the Divine Favor on the Society of the Atonement, and this solemn declaration on the part of the God of Abraham concerning "the immutability of His Counsel," divinely "confirmed by an oath" beyond the possibility of ultimate failure. Woe be unto us if, after this, we shall "fall away." Oh God, establish in us the truest humility and entire dependence on Thee, that our faith fail not!

In true scriptural tradition he wrote a hymn, the only one he ever composed, to celebrate what he believed to be the decisive intervention of God in his life. He would sing it throughout his life even when his enterprises faltered and others gave up hope.

THE COVENANT HYMN

O God, Who makest Covenant,
Whose promise Thou wilt never break,
Make strong Thy servants militant
With faith and love no pow'r can shake.
Thy word prevail, when foes assail,
Lest we should fail, lest we should fail.

"Fear not," saidst Thou to Abraham,
"For I will multiply thy seed;

Thy shield and great reward I am,
Believe and thou art blest indeed."
Thine oath recall, when hosts appall,
Lest we should fall, lest we should fall.

The night in which He was betrayed
Our Lord took bread, gave thanks and brake.
Likewise the cup when He had prayed,
"My Body 'tis, and Blood, partake."
This food supply, nor us deny,
Lest we should die, lest we should die.

What Thou hast pledged to pass must come,
Thou shalt "repair the breach" of old,
The "other sheep" with those of Rome,
Shall constitute one only Fold.
This pledge recall, when hosts appall,
Lest we should fall, lest we should fall.

All glory, Lord, to Thee we pay,
To Father, Son and Holy Ghost.
Thy will let men on earth obey
That they may join the Heavenly Host,
Thy word prevail, when foes assail,
Lest we should fail, lest we should fail.

Amen

Now the Society of the Atonement had a name and a covenant with God, but still it had no home. During his visit to "The Terrace," Sister Lurana had told Father Wattson of an incident that happened during her convent stay in London. One evening at Vespers she saw across the choir another visiting American nun like herself, but dressed in a religious habit unfamiliar to her. After the service she was introduced to Sister Mary Angela, a member of the Anglican Community of Saint Mary, Peekskill, New York. There was much "heavenly gossip" about their respective hopes and plans, and in later correspondence Sister Lurana told her new friend about Father Wattson and their ideas for a future Society of the Atonement. Sister Angela responded with a fascinating story about a local abandoned church which might serve as the site of the new enterprise. This was her account:

Three pious Anglican ladies had discovered a small abandoned chapel during their summer vacation in the Hudson highlands. Across the river from West Point, in the town of Garrison, they came upon the forlorn little building on a remote country lane during a carriage ride through the countryside. The chapel had not been used for religious services for at least ten years, but despite its isolation local tramps had found it convenient as a hobo hotel. The windows were broken, the door half smashed in, some of the furniture had been used for firewood, and the filth and dirt were appalling.

Like St. Francis of Assisi, who restored the ruined chapel of San Damiano in response to a heavenly vision, the three ladies got to work and cleaned up the worst of the mess as best they could. Then they went to the rector of the local Episcopal Church, St. Philip's in Garrison, who already knew about the abandoned building. He was uninterested in its future, but at their insistence reluctantly gave them permission to hold services there if they so desired. They got a chaplain to come up from New York to re-open their little country chapel, St. John's-in-the-Wilderness.

Not long after the re-opening, the church and the half acre of property on which it stood were offered to the good ladies who had restored it. They called the place "Graymoor" after the two persons most closely associated with its early days: Dr. Gray, one-time rector of the Garrison church who had built the chapel around 1878; and Mr. Moore, a professor at Columbia University who had been the chief benefactor. Since the ladies now had the full responsibility of caring for the church, they humorously called themselves "the vestry" of St. John's-in-the-Wilderness. By a strange coincidence, they had discovered the church in 1893, the same year Father Wattson discovered his atonement texts and the name of his future society.

Like Father Wattson and Sister Lurana, the ladies were devotees of St. Francis, and they gave the church a coat of brown paint over its original white in honor of the Poverello of Assisi. Wouldn't it be nice, they thought, if they could give the church to some group of nuns following the Franciscan Rule?

They must have brought their dreams to the attention of Sister Angela at her nearby Peekskill convent, who in turn urged Sister Lurana to accept the place. "I only hope Father Wattson may not discourage this idea," Sister Angela wrote, "but it is all being directed and ordered for you, no doubt, and I must trust it to the only One Who knows what is best for you and for His Glory."

So it was that Sister Lurana told Father Wattson about the little brown church in the dell during their retreat at Warwick. He was delighted, and he hastened to Graymoor at the close of the retreat. He arrived on October 10th, 1898. "Surely, they may exclaim," he said, "those happy souls whom God has called to this lovely place: 'I have a goodly heritage, my lot has fallen unto me in pleasant places,' for theirs is the 'hundredfold' promised even in this life to those who leave all to follow Christ."

Every gift God gave Father Wattson was always the

(left) *The Palace of Lady Poverty*

(below) *The friary at Graymoor*

best, in his estimation at least. The site of the little church at the end of a country lane, nestled at the foot of what would later become known as the "Mount of the Atonement," was a place so remote that even Wattson admitted that a letter addressed to "Graymoor" would end up in a dead-letter office. But no matter. God had undoubtedly reserved from all eternity this Mount, untouched by trace of previous habitation, as the site of his new foundation. It was the best of all possible sites because it was the gift of God.

Sister Lurana was anxious to go to Graymoor at once. She met with the three ladies of the "vestry," Miss Elliot, her sister Mrs. Nicholson, and Sister Mary Angela's cousin, Miss Redmond, who were overjoyed at the prospects.

A letter from Father Wattson arrived later in the fall. "Surely it is the Holy Spirit Who prompts you to go to Graymoor at once, and with gladness I bid you God's speed. The time of waiting is past. God's Advent message to you is 'Go forward,' and your joy is in Obedience. . . . 'May He send His angels before thy face to guide thee in all thy ways!' "

Sister Lurana left her home on December 15th, 1898, accompanied by her sister Annie White and a poor girl she had adopted as a godchild. This last leg of the journey was made by horse and sleigh through deep snow and bitter cold, a stark contrast to the autumn beauty of the scene Father Wattson had enjoyed a few months before. Sister Lurana had rented a farm cottage called "The Dimond House." It was more than a century old, and in many places the icy winds came through the crevices in the walls. They had to walk half a mile through the drifts to their country church, St. John's. That first night they swept out the old cottage, lighted a fire in the smokey stove and for supper shared a loaf of bread which had been given them by a poor woman that morning. The next morning Annie White departed, leaving Sister Lurana and her godchild to face the rigors of the desolate place alone.

Somehow they got through that dreadful winter, and in the spring the ground was broken for a new convent adjoining St. John's. Father Wattson couldn't be there for the dedication. He was "a prisoner in spiritual bonds" at the novitiate of the Episcopal Order of the Holy Cross in Westminster, Maryland, where he was learning to be a religious.

If Sister Lurana had put in a tough winter, so had Father Wattson. He had gone to one of the few religious orders of the Episcopal Church for his novitiate because all his previous knowledge of religious life came exclusively from books. He wanted to be trained in monastic discipline and he got what he requested. His novice master was an old classmate from General Theological Seminary, Henry Sargent. When he confided his dreams of the Society of the Atonement to his novice master, explaining that the institute would include friars, sisters, and lay tertiaries, the unimpressed Sargent replied "I don't believe you have a vocation to found one religious order, let alone three." Sargent, true to his name, was as tough a superior as Wattson himself had been in Omaha. Now the shoe was on the other foot, and Father Wattson was learning what it meant to take orders as well as give them.

Sargent even disapproved of novice Wattson's correspondence with Sister Lurana. He was subjected to penances and trials of every kind, the idea being that this was the way to train a religious. He wrote: "the hardest lesson I have to learn is patience. . . . After the almost incessant work of nearly fourteen years of ministerial service it is indeed a joyous thing to retire into the desert with St. John the Baptist and learn the ABC of the contemplative life. I feel that 'bonds and imprisonments await me' when I again put forth into the world to grapple with Satan in the stronghold of pride and rebellion against God. And, Oh, I do need to get down to the very roots of pride and self-will in my own nature and learn the truest and most profound humility. . . ."

He was still full of plans for the society. What would Sister Lurana think of a white habit for him to emphasize his witness to the celibate priesthood? Absolutely not, she replied, because future members must conform inwardly and outwardly to the Franciscan Rule. In this, as in many future decisions, he deferred to her.

Toward the end of September 1899, the sisters at Graymoor lost their commuting chaplain and Father Wattson decided that the time had come to leave his novitiate and begin his new life. On his way to Garrison he passed through the nation's capital where he visited the famous Franciscan Monastery of the Holy Land in Washington, D.C. He had read about Franciscans but had never talked to one. Unlike his former novice master, Father Sargent, the Roman Catholic Franciscans in Washington were kind and sympathetic to his plans. When he left the monastery, they gave him the blessing of St. Francis with all their heart, and Father Wattson never forgot this first personal contact with Roman Catholicism in its Franciscan manifestation.

On the eve of the feast of St. Francis of Assisi, October 3rd, 1899, Father Wattson alighted from the train at the little station in the town of Garrison. As he walked the dirt road to Graymoor, he was overtaken by a man riding in a buckboard, a local contractor who had just completed building Sister Lurana's new convent. Father Wattson asked if the man knew of any caves in the nearby hills that he might use as a hermit's cell. He had no money and no place to live, and as he told the startled contractor of his plans to literally imitate the example of St. Francis by living in complete poverty, the man offered him the use of an unused paint shack rather than see him spend the coming winter in a cave.

After a brief visit with Sister Lurana, Father Wattson and the contractor continued up the Mount of the Atonement to the top, where the contractor told him there was a beautiful river view. "Upon this mountain," he enthusiastically exclaimed, "will rise the monastery home of the preaching friars. From these heights the prayers and works of reparation of countless Friars of the Atonement shall daily ascend to the throne of the mighty Lord of heaven and earth, beseeching His mercy and clemency upon a sinful world." There was only one problem: he didn't own the place, but that seemed not to have disturbed him at all.

Sister Lurana had met a wealthy Englishwoman on the boat from England, who later donated the $300 which purchased the entire Mount. That donor became a companion of Sister Lurana's and died many years later as a member of the Graymoor community.

Father Wattson took possession of the property on June 14th, 1900, the Feast of Corpus Christi. He carried on his back a large wooden cross which he fashioned himself and set it up on top of his mountain where it stands to this day. Although Father Wattson was legally the owner, he considered himself only its trustee until that day when the Anglican Communion would be reunited with Rome, at which time the deed would be placed at the feet of St. Peter's successor as a token of fealty, obedience, and devotion.

The first monastery of the Friars of the Atonement was the unused paint shack loaned by the builder of the sisters' convent to Father Wattson. He dubbed it "The Palace of Lady Poverty." It was well named and when it rained he had to hold an umbrella in one hand and his breviary in the other. His only light was a candle, and he stuffed the holes in the walls with paper and rags. He wore an overcoat and boots constantly because of the cold.

Soon he assumed the gray-brown Franciscan habit designed for him by Sister Lurana. Since there was no one of authority in the Episcopal Church present, Father Wattson officiated at his own investiture after an all-night vigil. "It was with much fear and a sinking heart that I at last put on the habit about which I had so long dreamed," he wrote. "During that time of preparatory prayer and meditation a vision of what it meant to follow the Crucified was given to me. It was a foreshadowing of Gethsemane, and my poor heart and soul shrinks from the ordeal that lies before me. But I am very happy about it, nevertheless. Each day I am growing to love my habit more and more." To a modified version of the original Franciscan habit he added a crucifix on a red cord suspended around his neck.

From then on he wore the habit everywhere and soon became satisfied that he could "go anywhere in these United States without being a target for jibes and boisterous ridicule." He became a familiar figure not only in the neighborhood of Graymoor but in New York City as well, where he liked to preach from the steps of City Hall.

"Once a week I would stand on the City Hall steps, sing the hymn 'Tell Them the Wonderful Story,' and when a crowd gathered I would preach. My Franciscan habit, I was sure, would quickly draw an audience. Then a New York City policeman would give me a chair behind the columns and I would talk to anyone who wished to see me."

Now he was ready to make his official profession of the religious vows of poverty, chastity, and obedience. He asked the Bishop of Delaware, the Rt. Rev. Leighton Coleman, to come for the occasion. Since there were no buildings in which to hold the ceremony, he pitched a government suplus tent left over from the Spanish-American War on the summit of his Mount, next to the Corpus Christi Cross he had erected. He took the name "Paul" in religion, recalling his childhood dream of founding a preaching order. To this the bishop added "James," after the apostle whose feast day had occurred during the week of the profession ceremonies. Sister Lurana was disappointed that the bishop had not chosen "Francis," but Father Paul, as he was thereafter known, saw that James was the equivalent of Jacob the grandson of Abraham. "I am going to ask all the members of the Society present to come and kneel before me as the Patriarch Jacob asked his sons to do, that I may give you my blessing," he said after the ceremony. By another one of those numerical coincidences he found so significant in his life, the number of people who came forward for his blessings was twelve, the same as Jacob's sons. Some weeks later Father Paul received permission from the bishop to add Francis to his name, which he regarded as the family name of the friars and sisters. As the co-founder of the Society with Father Paul, Sister Lurana now became Mother Lurana Mary Francis, S.A.

Well schooled in Scripture, both Old and New, and in

the allegorical interpretations of the Fathers of the Christian Church, Father Paul often saw deeper meanings in what usually would be considered ordinary everyday occurrences. Moreover, he excelled in seeing striking parallels between historical events widely separated in time, and he extracted from them the last ounce of possible significance. Take, for example, his explanation of the name which Mother Lurana bore in the religious life:

When I say that she (Mother Lurana) was predestined to bear the name of the Atonement, I speak advisedly. In holy baptism she was given the name of Lurana Mary; and in the commencement of her life as a religious she still bore the name of Sister Lurana Mary. But when the time came for her profession at Graymoor in 1900, she wished to receive the name of Francis because of her great devotion and love for our Seraphic Father, St. Francis of Assisi. As the future Father General of the Society of the Atonement, whose profession took place on the Mount of the Atonement on July 27th in the same year, 1900, had received from the Anglican Bishop the name of Paul James, it did not seem fitting that the Mother General should receive three names, Lurana Mary Francis. Consequently it appeared necessary that either Mary or Lurana be dropped to make place for Francis. To discard the name of the Mother of God was unthinkable; the rejection of Lurana seemed inevitable, much as we regretted it.

The problem was happily solved by the Joint Founders of the Society of the Atonement both assuming with the permission of the bishop the name Francis. I further said to Mother: "Lurana must have a meaning; for God never gives a name without its having some significance." I tried my own wit and wisdom to discover what the significance was; but it was only after months of vain searching that the name came to me in a dream. Assisted by a New Testament Greek lexicon, on the feast of the Beheading of St. John the Baptist, August 29, 1901, I completed the discovery; . . *Lu*, the first syllable, means to loose, pardon or redeem—the second, *Ran*, means sprinkling and is used by both St. Peter and St. Paul of the Atonement Blood. So that Lurana in the New Testament Greek means "Redeemed by (the blood of) sprinkling, i.e., Atonement." After the Mother's profession had taken place on St. Francis Day, October 4th, 1900, while we were lunching together, one of the clergy present said to me: "This is Yom Kippur, the Day of Atonement." So without knowing it, the Mother Foundress was professed on the ancient day of the Atonement; and it was nearly a year later that she learned the significance of the name which she was the first to bear as a religious.

Mother Lurana had found a few followers who joined her community, as well as a number of lay people who became tertiaries. Father Paul's first friar was a young converted Jew, Ferdinand Wallerstein, who became Brother Anthony. He was Father Paul's only companion for years. Recruits were few for the little society and life was hard. A friend of Father Paul's wrote at the time of his death: "You ought to have seen Graymoor in the early days! No one in the world but Father Paul could have started 'from scratch,' without a nickel, and built up the glorious institution that now is a model for the church."

It must have taken a great deal of faith to see Graymoor as the cradle of a major religious institution in those days. At the top of the Mount, Father Paul had only the one permanent companion, although there was an ever-increasing stream of visitors. Few stayed very long in those austere conditions. One visitor in the early days was a brother of Father Paul, Charles Edward Wattson, who was as easy-going and informal as the founder of Graymoor was earnest and serious. One bleak early morning Charles was awakened at the crack of dawn by his brother, who announced: "Charles, this is a religious institution. You will have to get up like everyone else." Looking out of the window on the howling wilderness, Charles replied, "Well where the hell is the institution?" Others asked the same question, but to Father Paul the dream had already become a reality.

IV
"Though the Whole World Be Against Us"

NO SOONER HAD FATHER PAUL settled in his palace of Lady Poverty at Graymoor than he began to wrestle anew with the problem of Roman primacy. In a conference with Mother Lurana in the summer of 1900 he outlined what he now recognized as the vocation of the society. Its members were obliged to witness to Roman primacy before Anglicans wherever and whenever they might be found, to denounce Henry VIII's breach with Rome and to preach corporate reunion of the worldwide Anglican communion with the Roman Catholic Church.

The two founders had good cause to pause for reflection. What would be the result of such a witness in an age when sectarian controversy was bitter and at times even physically violent? How could a fledgling little Anglican religious community barely off the ground possibly survive the certain onslaught it would have to suffer when it unveiled its program of Roman Catholic propaganda within the Anglican Church? "Do you realize to what persecutions, ostracism, and peril of annihilation you will be exposing the Society of the Atonement by undertaking such a propaganda?" she asked. "Yes," he answered, "I think I do realize quite clearly what a wild and foolhardy proposal it is from the standpoint of worldly prudence. As far as I know, I am the only Anglican ecclesiastic in 30,000 who holds these views; nevertheless, if our witness is from God, sooner or later it will prevail, though the whole world be against us."

"With eyes wide open, therefore, to the consequences, and putting present popularity behind them," Father Paul wrote, "the joint Founders of the Graymoor Institute determined to plant their feet firmly on the Rock of Peter and courageously face the storm, which they felt morally certain would sooner or later overtake the infant Society of the Atonement." Their predictions were not mistaken.

Shortly after, Father Paul had two Anglican visitors, one a rector in whose church he had recently conducted a mission. After proudly showing off the new convent and St. John's Church, Father Paul invited them to trudge up the mountain for a visit to the site of his new monastery, still a trackless wilderness. As they reached the summit and looked out over the Hudson Valley below, Father Paul revealed to his horrified Anglican guests his recently determined policy for Graymoor. What had Anglican controversialists since the Reformation done, after all, but to build up a system of Catholicism with the pope left out? he asked. His study of Scripture, tradition, and history convinced him that the papacy was by Divine right the visible center of the Church. The Anglican position about Rome always had been wrong, and would never be right again until the *Ecclesia Anglicana* made its submission to the jurisdiction of the Holy See.

All the way down the mountainside the guests argued with Father Paul to no avail. When they reached the bottom they parted company in more ways than one.

Modern Roman Catholic piety has dubbed St. Jude the Apostle the patron of the impossible. Whether Father Paul knew this or not, he chose the saint's feast day, October 28th, 1900, to commit his society to its Roman position. Gathering his little community before him in St. John's Church he preached a fiery sermon based on a text from the Epistle of St. Jude, "Dearly beloved, I beseech you to contend earnestly for the Faith once for all delivered to the Saints." That "faith," Father Paul said with great emotion, "is the faith of the Holy Roman Church, and the Chair of Peter at Rome is the divinely constituted center of a reunited Christendom." He then called the members of the community one by one into the convent next door where he called upon them to sign their names to a declaration of faith he himself had drawn up embodying the main points of his sermon. Those who declined to sign were automatically dropped from the membership roles. So there it was: the impossible task had been irrevocably taken up. A handful of eccentric Anglicans living in a wilderness were determined to undo the effects of the whole English Reformation. St. Jude was a likely patron indeed.

Three months later Father Paul tried his Roman propaganda on another visitor. A legacy left to Mother Lurana by her grandmother had been used to erect a small friary on the top of the mountain for Father Paul and his one companion, Brother Anthony. The society's ecclesiastical visitator, Bishop Coleman of Delaware, was invited to officiate at its dedication on December 8th, the feast of the Immaculate Conception in the Roman Calendar. Father Paul announced in the bishop's presence that the new building would be dedicated in honor of the dogma of the Immaculate Conception. This the bishop accepted without visible protest, but after the ceremonies when Father Paul outlined the Roman position the society now held, Bishop Coleman asked for time to pray over the matter. In a few days he sent a letter saying that although he did not personally believe in the Immaculate Conception or the infallibility of the pope, he would not at this time withdraw as episcopal visitator of the society.

Father Paul's fiery Romanism became widely known, and in the summer of 1901 he was invited to preach in St. Barnabas's Church in Brooklyn, New York by its Catholic-minded rector. Not content with preaching indoors, he went into a nearby square where his Franciscan habit, as usual, attracted a crowd. The *Brooklyn Citizen* devoted three columns to the event under the banner "To Unite Roman and Anglican," and carried a partial text of his sermon:

There is scarce a band, or company of creatures in God's universe, from the denizens of the beehive to the choirs of angels in heaven itself, who do not possess one of their number to act as leader and preserve unity. In legislative bodies not so much as a committee of three can discharge its functions unless one of the three presides in a chair of unity. It is a madman's dream to contemplate a united church on earth without a visible head. If every parish must have its rector, and every diocese its bishop, and every province its archbishop, how could the whole Catholic Church throughout the world exist as one fold without having one supreme or chief shepherd over all? . . ."

That fall, to further propagate his ideas, he founded The Rosary League of Our Lady of the Atonement, whose organ was a tiny periodical entitled *Rose Leaves from Our Lady's Garden at Graymoor*. The league's purpose was to pray for restoration of England, Mary's Dowry, as it was known in medieval times, because of its devotion to the Mother of God and its Catholic allegiance. In the first issue the editor wrote: "May we hope that *Rose Leaves from Our Lady's Garden* will be treasured by those who receive the little paper, not only because of the witness it bears to Catholic truth and the honor of the Mother of God, but also because it is a monthly visitor from Graymoor, the Beulah Land of the Atonement."

During 1908 in *Rose Leaves*, Paul wrote:

After the breach with Rome in the sixteenth century, the two truths which the Devil struck at most strongly in the English Church were the worship of Christ in the Mass and the devotion to the Blessed Mother of God. In the present time, when the walls of the vineyard are being assaulted by those from within, who seek through "open pulpit" canons and other devices to let into the Church by wholesale heretical teachers who scorn a sacrificial priesthood and deny a supernatural religion, we ought to recognize, with clearest vision, that increased devotion to Jesus, present in the Mass, and to the Holy Rosary of Our Lady, are the two principal weapons by which we resist the gates of hell and confound the wicked one.

No wonder Father Paul, Anglican, was in trouble with

his Church! It was words like these that made the blood of most Episcopalians boil. *Indeed*, "the Blessed Mother of God" and "the Holy Rosary of Our Lady"! In those days few good members of the Protestant Episcopal Church in the United States would have entertained the thought that devotion to Mary and the Rosary was one of "the two principal weapons" in the defeat of Satan. More likely, they would have considered such devotions diabolically inspired aberrations.

As we have seen so often in his life, for Father Paul it was a matter of all or nothing in the instance of Saint Mary, too. Since he was already proclaiming the need for Anglicans to recognize the primacy of the pope in the Church and to unite themselves corporately with the Church of Rome, it should come as no surprise that Father Paul the Anglican would also have a good deal to say to his fellow churchmen about Saint Mary and Marian devotions. Long before 1908 Father Paul had had an interest in, and perhaps even a devotion to Saint Mary.

This devotional peculiarity, at least for an Anglican, was of course very much in line with the doctrinal and liturgical beliefs and practices of the tiny Anglo-Catholic movement within the American Protestant Episcopal Church. To be sure, the New York "cathedral" of the High Church party on the Eastern seaboard of the United States was even called "St. Mary the Virgin," a name which was an insult to some of the more evangelical churchmen. For the latter, there was no doubt that the word "Protestant" in the official title of their Church meant eschewing any and all such "papist" nonsense.

In one of the first issues of *Rose Leaves*, the startling announcement was made that "in her wonderful conde-

Lewis Wattson as an Anglican priest

scension and love the Mother of God has been pleased to reveal herself to the Children of the Atonement under a new name, thus giving remarkable evidence that the honor, love and prayers addressed to her, as Our Lady of the Atonement, she is graciously pleased to accept."

Not only was Father Paul willing to promote Marian devotion and even give Saint Mary a new name under the title of the Atonement but he also propagandized the very doctrines of the Roman Church concerning her, namely the Immaculate Conception and the Assumption, which to Protestants and Anglicans must have seemed the most theologically outrageous of all. Near the end of 1904 Paul wrote an article about the Assumption of Mary in which he said: "The theological reasons for accepting the doctrine of the Assumption are overwhelming in their cogency. It is unthinkable to any devout and reverent mind that our Lord would permit the body of His Mother, which He had hallowed by His Incarnate Life, to become food for worms in the corruption of the grave. . . ."

Admitting that there is little in Scripture and nothing in history about the fact of the Assumption, Father Paul appealed to the standard Roman arguments when he wrote that "it would be contrary to the whole analogy of Divine Revelation to expect detailed historical evidences for the resurrection of the body of the Blessed Virgin by the power and love of her divine Son. Such a manifestation of His love for her is a sacred mystery of His Incarnation that immediately concerns what we reverently term His private relation to her, and not the public relation of His Incarnate Life to redeemed humanity in general." How widely read in Roman theological literature and how strange Father Paul must have seemed to most Anglicans becomes apparent when it is remembered that even the Roman Church did not proclaim the dogma of the Assumption as infallible doctrine until nearly 50 years after Paul's article was written in 1904. As in so many other aspects of his life, here also Paul was an extremist, perhaps in a gallant effort to show his opponents that he was really and truly a Catholic, indeed a papist of the papists. For an Anglican, of course, this was an absurd type of ultramontanism, a blatant denial of all it meant to be an Anglican.

Not only was Paul a proponent of the Assumption of Saint Mary but he also had a good deal to say about her Immaculate Conception even while he was an Anglican. During the same year in which he wrote about Saint Mary's Assumption, he was bold enough to say the following:

The Anglican who pays scant respect to the Holy Mother of God; never says a Hail Mary; has no use for the Rosary; and rejects as false the dogma of the Immaculate Conception, is recreant to the oldest and most hallowed traditions of the Anglican Communion. . . . That this dogma is no new thing, invented by Pope Pius IX, no one ought to know better than those who call themselves English Catholics. The greatest theological champion the dogma ever had . . . was an Oxford professor, who flourished six hundred years ago, the Franciscan doctor, John Duns Scotus. . . .

No less was Father Paul devoted to the practice of the Rosary. As we have seen, one of the first organizations which the founders began was the Rosary League. Explaining how the rosary was connected with the purpose of the society and of the league as well, Paul wrote that "without prayer we can do nothing and the design of the Rosary League is to surround the Society of the Atonement with an army of faithful auxiliaries, who recite the prayers of the Society . . . because we think Our Lady herself desires to be invoked and honored under this new name; and that she will grant special favors to those who have recourse to her under the salutation of Our Lady of the Atonement."

The new title for Saint Mary came, of course, from the name of the society he founded. How fond Paul was of making connections between Saint Mary and the Society of the Atonement can be seen from a letter written to a friend late in the founder's life: "Hardly any very important thing has happened in connection with the Society of the Atonement but what the major event fell on some feast of the Blessed Virgin. It was on the Feast of Our Lady's Nativity that the ground was broken, for example, for the Mother House of the Friars of the Atonement. . . . It was on the Octave of the Feast of the Visitation of the Blessed Virgin that I received the name of the society, while Rector of an Anglican Church in Kingston, New York. It was on the Octave of the Feast of the Immaculate Conception when our Mother Foundress came to Graymoor to make her Foundation." These were no mere coincidences for the founder, but unimpeachable signs that the hands of God and Saint Mary were working directly within the life of the Society of the Atonement.

While the community was still Anglican, a series of unusual events took place at Graymoor, occurrences which Paul apparently believed were of supernatural origin. These are what he called "The Three Apparitions." The "apparitions" are reported here exactly as recorded in official publications of the society.

The August 1905 issue of *Rose Leaves* contains the

earliest published account of the first of the three "apparitions," and the story runs as follows:

There are more than half a dozen events in the history of our Foundation of a character inexplicable upon any other than a supernatural basis. We hesitate even to refer to these, and yet one, at least, is so intimately bound up with the Society's devotion to the Holy Mother under the invocation of "Our Lady of the Atonement" that to omit all reference to it would to a few who read these notes leave a sense of loss and almost of unreality. Before going on to relate the occurrence we think it right to say that, grateful as we certainly are to God for this and the several other occurrences which assisted our faith and comforted us at critical moments in our history, still we do not feel that we have been either desirous of them, credulous when they were granted, or unduly influenced by them. . . .

It was Sunday evening in the Octave of All Saints, 1900. For reasons which we may not now go into, it had been for some days a time of grave anxiety for the little company of Sisters in St. Francis' House, and to our Mother especially there was not wanting the danger of even possible physical violence. Vespers of the Festival had been sung and the Benediction was over. Our Mother was kneeling in Chapel by a window overlooking the Sacristy door opening out of doors. Suddenly she heard the sound of crying, and glancing out of the window saw the little acolyte John (Hastings), still in his red cassock and, as we have just said, weeping. Hastening out to him, the Mother put her arms around him and said: "Why Johnnie! What is the matter?" He replied: "I just saw something."

Surprised, the Mother questioned: "What did you see, and what are you crying about?" Still sobbing, he managed to say: "I just saw Our Lady, and I am crying because I was so surprised." The Mother was rather incredulous for some time and questioned him very closely as to how he knew the appearance he believed he had seen was Our Lady; just where he saw her, how she looked, etc. Every time he repeated the same description: "She was large and very beautiful; he knew it was Our Lady, for she had the Christ Child in her arms; she appeared suddenly at the very moment the ostensorium was raised; she was on the Gospel side, right near where he was kneeling." The child's evident surprise and excitement and yet his positive assertions, impossible of simulation, even had he been that kind of child, which he was not, finally convinced us of the reality of the apparition; and a few days later a guest at the Friary, hearing the account, gave us the present of a very beautiful Munich statue of Our Lady to commemorate it. We are quite ready to believe and be consoled with the thought that our dear Mother came that night to assure her Children of the Atonement, and to tell them to fear nothing—though she was visible only to a little child.

The second "apparition" occurred less than a year later in 1901. One Amy Evans, later to be Sister Amelia, S.A., had just arrived at Graymoor to be a postulant and was living at the time in the garret of the convent where all the postulants stayed in dormitories partitioned by curtains. Her written statement of what happened on a night early in February, 1901, was produced under oath and printed in the October, 1914, issue of *The Lamp*. It runs as follows:

One night in February, 1901, I was awakened after I had been in bed a short time. At first I thought I had been called by the house caller, but when I opened my eyes the cell was light (but not daylight) and in the opposite corner stood a most beautiful lady. She had on a blue tunic and red mantle, in her left hand she had a heart which she was holding toward me. My first thought was, "I was dreaming," but when she disappeared the cell was in darkness and I lay awake some time, but feeling sure it was Our Lady who had come to show me she loved me and I was to love her more. I had never seen her represented as I saw her that night nor have I seen her since and have always been looking for a card or painting like it.

Eventually Sister Amelia would indeed see a card or

painting like the "apparition" she reported she saw that night, for the usual representation of Our Lady of the Atonement is exactly as she described, but instead of a heart Saint Mary holds forth the Christ Child with a cross in His hand.

In the winter of 1905, a local Methodist minister came to St. Paul's friary for a stay of a few months. Day after day, during his visit, Father Paul attempted to convince him of the truth of Roman claims about papal primacy. Finally, without having much success, the founder challenged him to join in prayer with the friars, asking God to give three signs as evidence of the truth of Roman doctrines. The next night upon retiring the minister saw a luminous cross hanging on the wall close to his bed. He put forth his hand to touch it, and to his amazement he found that the cross had no substance. This was the first sign.

One night later, the minister had a dream in which he saw capital and labor pitted against one another in a fight to the finish. Suddenly there appeared between the hostile opponents a procession of Franciscan friars led by a banner-bearer. Upon the exhortation of the friars' leader, the combatants threw down their arms and embraced each other in fraternal brotherhood. This was the second sign.

On March 4th, 1905, Father Paul wrote the following in his notebook:

On this night (Saturday), while Edward and Gordon Gregory were saying night prayers in Chapel, there being no light but the sanctuary lamp, Gordon saw a large white cross from ceiling to floor on which hung Our Lord, and Our Lady knelt to the left (Epistle) side, a round white globe between her and the foot of the cross. This Gordon told immediately on coming out to the Father and returning he still saw the Crucified One, though fainter, and Our Lady had disappeared.

This was the third sign. The Methodist minister never became a Roman Catholic, however, but returned to Jersey City where he lived happily ever after.

While these "apparitions" may not appear too impressive in themselves, especially to modern Christians, they are expressive of a certain type of spirituality for which Father Paul felt a strange affinity. He did, after all, believe that the "apparitions" really did take place, and many years later he used them as examples in his sermons on the nature of the divine plan for the Society of the Atonement. That such "apparitions" had occurred so early in the history of the society was, he believed, one more sign that God had divinely ordained that the community should come into existence as a late-comer to meet a very special need of the Church and the world. The hand of God was everywhere for Father Paul. "Apparitions," then, were continuing signs of divine ratification for what Paul was doing and a confirmation of the covenant which he felt God had made with him and Mother Lurana.

All of this was a far cry from the religious ethos of the average Episcopalian. Father Paul's insistent devotion to the Blessed Virgin, the use of the Rosary, the invocation of saints, and the re-creation of a whole spirituality more representative of medieval Catholicism than contemporary Anglicanism, all served to separate him from the mainstream of his own Church. But it was his persistent papalism that put him outside the pale. Episcopalians had long prided themselves as a comprehensive Church, but papalism seemed a threat to its very integrity.

When Father Paul preached his famous sermon about this time on Long Island, which was recounted in our first chapter, the *Living Church* editorialized in its issue of October 5th, 1901:

Whether there ever can be again . . . a universal Primacy on the part of the See of Rome may be an abstract question upon which men may legitimately differ. It is at present of the practical value of the celebrated problem as to who killed Cock Robin. We regret that an esteemed one of our clergy should have taken this unfortunate position which cannot fail seriously to mar his influence. We feel that he stands absolutely alone in his position, and that it is wholly inconsistent with the ecclesiastical allegiance which he owes to his bishop and the national Church. . . . The whole Anglican communion is unanimous in repudiating absolutely the doctrine of Papal Supremacy, which the earnest but erratic priest of Graymoor has preached.

Now he was a national issue, and every pulpit of the Episcopal Church was closed to him. Shut out of the churches, he continued to preach out-of-doors, but his papalism was as unacceptable to Roman Catholics as it was offensive to his fellow Anglicans because of his insistence on corporate reunion. Every individual conversion to the Church of Rome, he contended, was a disloyalty to the general welfare of the Anglican Church. When two friends who had recently become Roman Catholics visited him and suggested he make his individual submission to the pope, he defended the principle of corporate reunion by saying: "You tell me to go to Rome. My father was told to do the same thing. The Oxford men were told to do the same thing. If they had taken the advice given to them there would be no Catholic Revival in the Episcopal Church. If *they* had gone to Rome you would not be here today advising me to follow you. There must be something more than a conviction that Rome is right. There must be a conviction that it is right for me to go to Rome now. *I have no such conviction.* To me it seems that there should be a *corporate reunion,* and this is being delayed by individual conversions."

There was only one way for one born outside of the Roman Catholic communion to achieve Church membership in Father Paul's day. Converts to the Church were required, as ordained by the decrees of the post-Reformation Council of Trent, to individually take a public oath that they abjured, detested and abhorred every heresy and sect opposed to the one Holy Catholic Apostolic and Roman Church, and to be absolved from excommunication. Even their baptism was considered doubtful, and in most cases conditional rebaptism was required. The only thing the convert could bring to Catholicism was repentance. He was to shake off the dust of any previous Christian association from the hem of his garment and the soles of his feet before entering St. Peter's Bark.

So Father Paul's position was equally at odds with both Roman Catholicism and Anglicanism as understood in his day. He was tragically caught betwixt and between. To Anglicans he was a traitorous renegade. To Romans he had not yet humbled himself and been sufficiently purified of former associations to be acceptable even as a prospective member. He was a man without a Church who loved the Church.

Looking back on his cruel dilemma it is interesting to note a current change in Roman Catholic practice in this regard. A new 1974 "Rite of Reception of Baptized Christians into Full Communion with the Catholic Church" now notes that the term "convert" may not be appropriately applied to Christians coming to Roman Catholicism from another Church. Rather that term refers only to one who comes from unbelief to Christian belief, and not to "a subsequent change of Christian communion." The new rite no longer calls for abjuration of error or absolution from excommunication, but only for a simple profession of faith and a declaration of reception by the priest.

On the feast of Candlemas, on February 2nd, 1903, Father Paul founded what was to become the longest lived of his many literary enterprises. *The Lamp*, a monthly magazine devoted to Christian unity, gave that forum for his views denied him in Anglican pulpits. Its first issue quoted Isaiah 62 verse 1, "For Zion's sake will I not hold my peace, and for Jerusalem's sake I will not rest, until the righteousness thereof go forth as brightness, and the salvation thereof as a lamp that burneth." *The Lamp* burned for 71 years until rising printing costs extinguished it in 1974. On every page it carried, first in Latin and later in English, the words: "That All May Be One."

Early issues continued to hammer away with his pro-Roman propaganda, yet amidst all the polemics and the tension of what surely must have seemed to be an impossible position, a serene sense of faith prevailed. In the first issue he wrote these words, perhaps the best summation of his hopes and dreams.

Is then Church Unity a visionary dream? Will the prayer of the Son of God never be answered? Was He a lying Prophet when He foretold the time of its fulfillment, saying: "Other sheep I have, which are not of this Fold (the one, Catholic and Apostolic Church), them also I must bring and there shall be one Fold and one Shepherd." Let who will deride or shake their heads in doubt, saying: "Heresy and schism have gone too far; the seamless Robe of CHRIST is too much torn to tatters ever to be mended; the Reunion of Christendom is utterly out of the question; Rome is too proud and unbending; England is too self-satisfied; the East too orthodox; Protestantism too much enamoured of letting everybody do and think just as they please. They never can and they never will come together. Church Unity is hopeless!" Our answer is, God's Will is Omnipotent; the Fiat of the Most High must prevail; the Prayer of JESUS CHRIST has got to be answered; the Almighty FATHER would never refuse the dying request of His only Begotten SON; sooner or later every petition of CHRIST will inevitably be granted. Were the mountains of difficulty to be surmounted a thousand times higher and vaster than they are GOD is able to cast them into the sea. Faith serenely rests her case with HIM.

Yet even Faith must "Tarry the Lord's leisure," for with God 'a thousand years are but as one day.' Patience must be allowed plenty of time in which to do her work perfectly. She cannot and she will not be hurried, the fabric is exceedingly delicate, the pattern most elaborate, The Robe of Unity she is weaving for her SON of GOD will be of matchless beauty, but it is the work of many generations and Hope with smiling countenance kneels and prays, being quite happy and content to wait. And Love standing between the two looks over the shoulder of Patience and cheers her on saying, "Be of good courage, my sister, He, the Desire of all nations, will come and will not tarry and behold His reward is with Him."

He needed faith to sustain him as month after month letters to the editor of *The Lamp* came in with little encouragement and a great deal of criticism. An Episcopal clergyman wrote, "Your position is absolutely untenable. It is neither Anglican nor Roman, and I am positive, therefore, that it cannot be Catholic." A prominent Jesuit writing in the *Sacred Heart Messenger* exclaimed, "How anyone can pretend to obey the Pope and remain an Anglican is more than we can understand." Father Paul and Mother Lurana thought they would like to start a local chapter of the League of the Sacred Heart, but its Jesuit sponsors would have none of that. They wrote Father Paul that those "outside the pale of salvation were ineligible for membership." The Graymoor founders were deeply hurt.

In a series of articles entitled "Our Divided Allegiance," Father Paul attempted to defend his seemingly untenable position.

In all good conscience before God, we conceive our spiritual allegiance to be a divided one; not, we hope, through any grievous fault of our own but because, long before we were born, two things which God has joined together, man, in the violence of self-will and evil passion, unlawfully put asunder. When father and mother quarrel and separate, the children are of necessity confronted with a divided allegiance . . . there being schism in the household the children, in a measure, become a law unto themselves and balance their allegiance to either parent as wisely as they may. . . . Our spiritual Mother (the Anglican Church) and the Father of Christendom were alienated from one another three hundred seventy years ago; as dutiful children of both we desire to render to each the love and obedience which our conscience, enlightened by the Holy Spirit, dictates. Herein lies at the same time our peace and our tribulation. . . . Terribly crippled as the Church of England is by reason of heresy and schism we do most lovingly confess and acknowledge her to be our spiritual mother. Yes, and we are sure God, our Saviour, loves her too with a love fathomless as the ocean, deathless as Himself, and all the while He is leading her back, step by step, patiently, tenderly, through the long night back to the Father's House.

And we, the sons and daughters . . . will cling to her always. . . . When the mother, pardoned and reconciled, dwells once more in the Father's House we will dwell there too, most gladly, most joyfully; but we would rather be with her in the desert, fighting her battles and helping our Lord bring her on the homeward way, yes, to die in exile by her side, than disowning her to herd with Peter's sheep, though it were in the greenest pasture and to "lie down beside the still waters of comfort."

There could be no divided loyalty in the Roman Catholic Church of that day. There was only one true Church. Pope Leo was in it and Father Paul was out of it. Years later, Vatican Council II took a more lenient view, however. Its Decree on Ecumenism, while continuing to emphasize the real differences which separate Roman Catholics from other Christians, ascribed real theological significance to other Churches. It declares as follows:

The brethren divided from us also carry out many of the sacred actions of the Christian religion. Undoubtedly, in ways that vary according to the conditions of each Church or Community, these actions can truly engender a life of grace, and can be rightly described as capable of providing access to the community of salvation. It follows that these separated Churches and Communities, though we believe they suffer from defects already mentioned, have by no means been deprived of significance and importance in the mystery of salvation.

In Father Paul's day the Roman Catholic Church saw those outside its fold only as individuals. In our own day it has come to grips with the collective reality in theological terms of groups separated from itself. Thus while the language of the Second Vatican Council is still not overly complimentary in its assessment of other Christian Churches, it does recognize them as instruments of salvation and ecclesial realities. Consequently, the door has been opened for a dialogue between the Roman Catholic Church and the Churches separated from it. It is for this reason that Pope Paul can speak of the Anglican communion as "Our Sister Church" despite the differences which still remain. Such amity was impossible for Father Paul.

Edward Hawks was an Anglican friend of Father Paul's who later became a Roman Catholic. He recalled in his memoirs how *The Lamp* caused havoc at his high church Episcopal seminary in Wisconsin, Nashotah House. "The first copies that reached the reading room at Nashotah were torn up and the students were furious." But the magazine brought to Episcopalians a line of argument they had never seen before because they did not read Roman Catholic authors. In the days before the dialogue, whatever force Roman claims could have were magnified by their sudden descent upon Anglican minds utterly innocent of apologetical arguments for the primacy of Peter. The harlot of Babylon was shamelessly depicted as the Prince of the Apostles. The very audacity of such theological argument guaranteed an avid audience.

Anglicans might resent Father Paul but they couldn't ignore him. The *Church Standard*, Episcopal weekly of Philadelphia, noted in its March 23rd, 1903 issue that Father Paul did not sign his articles in *The Lamp*. "Anonymous traitors to the Church," it thundered ". . . must be left to their own secret devices." An Episcopal rector from Portsmouth, New Hampshire, wrote, "I beg to return this sheet, (*The Lamp*) I wish to have no part with such base unpardonable disloyalty. I utterly repudiate your avowed purpose and I brand you a dishonourable and dishonest son of Mother Church—without honour and without shame." The paid subscribers were few, and it was only by sending the sisters out to beg alms that Mother Lurana managed to finance the publication.

Meanwhile pressure was brought to bear on Bishop Coleman, episcopal visitator of Graymoor, to depose Father Paul as a heretic. *The New York Herald* of April 20th, 1903, carried the headline, "Father Paul, Episcopal Monk to be Tried for Declaring Reformation a Mistake." Recalling

Father Paul and Spencer Jones

Bishop Coleman's visit to Graymoor three years previously to witness his religious profession, Father Paul was quoted in the paper as saying "This is the Corpus Christi cross and here Bishop Coleman and I stood three years ago . . . here to this quiet spot I came as a witness to a great truth and I am ready for anything—for trial, for martyrdom if need be. Ostracized by the clergy, insulted by man and often reviled, I believe that some day, perhaps not in mine, all the Christian Churches will be united under the Bishop of Rome."

The trial never took place, perhaps in part because Father Paul impressed Bishop Coleman with his argument that, rather than denying any article of Anglican faith, his crime was that he believed more than was previously declared necessary for Anglicans.

A further weakening of Father Paul's position in the Anglican Church came in 1907 when the General Convention authorized bishops and rectors to invite non-Anglican preachers into their pulpits. In our ecumenical age this would seem to be a reasonable and progressive step, but to a man of Father Paul's churchmanship it was a recipe for speedy disaster. To him the Church was a teaching authority whose ministers, descended in an unbroken line of ordination from the apostles, taught the truths entrusted to the Church by Christ with divine authority. Only those in Holy Orders, commissioned by Christ to teach all nations, could legitimately and authoritiatively proclaim pure Catholic doctrine. In other words, the Church was not a forum but a teaching authority.

To many Anglo-Catholics the step of the General Convention, known as the "Open Pulpit Movement," was a direct threat to the Catholic character of the Church. It seemed to place nonordained on an equal footing with ordained, Catholic with Protestant, Orthodox with heterodox. As distinct from that speculative theological debate which might take place in a university, the pulpit of the parish church was the place where the faithful were taught sound Catholic doctrine.

The year 1907 came at the height of what was then known in Roman Catholic circles as the "Modernist Controversy," a bitter debate about such questions as the literal truth of the Scriptures, what place scholarly criticism should have in the evaluation of the Bible, whether modern trends of German philosophy should be integrated into the teaching of theology, and how far contemporary historical criticism should be allowed to interpret the progress of Church history. Pope Pius X and his supporters utterly defeated any attempt within the Roman Catholic Church to accommodate Catholic teaching to contemporary intellectual trends. Within Anglicanism a similar debate raged, although in this case adherence of all shades of opinion continued to live within one communion. Modernists came to be known as the "broad Church," sometimes erroneously thought of as a middle ground betwen low evangelicals and high Anglo-Catholics. As a matter of fact, Anglican evangelicals and Catholics had far more in common with each other than either did with free-wheeling broad churchmen who desired to accommodate Christian teaching to contemporary thought. Evangelicals on the contrary insisted on the pure faith of the Reformation, while Catholics harked back to the changeless character of the Church as exemplified in the patristic period.

Thus while Pius X was condemning modernism in the Decree of the Holy Office, *"Lamentabili"* in July 1907 and by the papal encyclical *"Pascendi"* in September of the same year, the Episcopal Church in the United States was inviting modernists into its pulpits. From the vantage point of our present-day views, we can perhaps see something in the stand of both sides in the controversy. Had the Church allowed itself to be indiscriminately conformed to the passing trends of the turn of the century it would find itself today not only cut loose from its anchor of orthodoxy and drifting in an unchartered sea but totally outdated and irrelevant to the trends and demands of our day as well. The Church seeks to transform the world, not the other way around.

What was sad about the whole affair was the high price the Roman Catholic Church paid for its purge of heterodoxy. What would now be considered legitimate methods of biblical and theological scholarship within the Church were excluded and did not find their rightful place within the context of Roman Catholic teaching until the Second Vatican Council.

Denied this hindsight vision of ours, Father Paul with other Anglo-Catholics denounced the open pulpit movement in the Episcopal Church as a disaster. He saw the act of the General Convention as an act of treason, a sell-out to heresy, a surrender to the very satanic forces Pius X was so vigorously resisting at that very moment. The Roman Catholic Church was going one way and the American Episcopal Church was going in the opposite direction, or so it seemed in 1907.

By the next year more than 20 priests and hundreds of lay people left the Episcopal Church for the Roman. Among these was Father William McGarvey, superior of a religious community known as the Companions of the

Holy Savior. Founded in 1891, the group of clergymen followed a simple rule, although this group did not desire nor display the elements of monastic life which Father Paul envisioned for his community. On May 27th, 1908, seven of the Companions of the Holy Savior entered the Roman Catholic Church, but it is interesting to note in the light of subsequent events that, although they acted as a group, the Roman Catholic Church would only receive them as individuals, and the Companions of the Holy Savior ceased to exist as a religious association.

At his Graymoor monastery Father Paul followed these events with agonized concern. "Until very lately," he wrote in *The Lamp*, "Episcopalians, like Roman Catholics, held themselves aloof. Their church, they said, was founded by Jesus Christ and not by Luther or Calvin or John Knox. . . ." Now the bishops had substituted comprehensiveness for catholicity, opening the gates of the "garden enclosed" to the "wild beasts of the field." His judgment on his Church was harsh and bitter. "A fountain that is poisoned at its source cannot but bring forth poisoned waters and that our Episcopate is certainly tinctured with the deadly poison of this bogus catholicity, commonly called Anglican Comprehensiveness, grows increasingly apparent from month to month. Something like a mania to decatholicise the Episcopal Church in the interests of Protestant Christianity seems to have gotten possession of the Anglican Episcopate the world over."

Many Protestants believed that they saw a new liberal spirit in the Episcopal Church that was attractive to them. The Episcopal *Living Church* opened its pages to a prominent Congregational minister who declared: "There is coming and to come a new Catholicism for our Protestant faith. The signs of its presence are such as these: One is the growth of a common Christian conscience. For us now no one church, no single church in existence, is big enough to hold a big Christian man." Father Paul replied in *The Lamp*: "If not one of the Churches already in existence is big enough, not even the Holy Roman Church, to contain one of 'the big Christian men', who are going to embrace it then? May the good Lord deliver us Lilliputians from their company lest we be crushed by their huge bulk."

His answer to the open pulpit was the formation in February of 1908 of the Anglo-Roman Union. One night the group met quietly for dinner in New York, hoping to avoid all publicity until the organization had acquired sufficient strength to withstand the opposition it was bound to provoke. But the *New York Sun* sniffed out the story and the following morning carried the headline "Pro-Roman Episcopalians Unite to Hail the Pope as Primate." It carried the names of those at the meeting. Describing Father Paul as the genius behind the movement and suggesting that such ideas were gaining ground rapidly, the story went on: "Evidences of a trend towards his teachings are said to have appeared in half of the Episcopal dioceses of the United States. The work has been carried on without display, and even now 'Father Paul' as he is usually called, deplores the publicity which his plans have gained."

Now it was out in the open. To some it seemed that Father Paul and the small company of like-minded Anglo-Catholics associated with him constituted a conspiracy to undermine the independence of Anglicanism from Rome. Once again Father Paul, like his father before him, appeared to be a "Jesuit in disguise."

As far as anyone could see, Paul Wattson had now

traveled his long road of developing loyalty to Roman claims within the Anglican Church to its very end. Every pulpit was closed to him. No magazine but his own would print his views. Visitors to his monastery had become few since his extreme Roman stand became known. Anglicans and Roman Catholics alike questioned the sincerity of his seemingly impossible attempt to unite two warring Churches in his own frail person.

What seemed impossible for man to accomplish was possible to Almighty God. Frustrated at every turn he now founded a prayer movement for the reunion of Christians which was to become his most widely known contribution to the whole Church.

About the turn of the century, Father Paul began a correspondence with an English clergyman by the name of Spencer Jones, and their letters developed into a book which they jointly published under the title *The Prince of the Apostles*. Although Father Paul and Father Jones were listed on the title page as co-authors, Mother Lurana contributed much to the book. She wrote the opening chapter and had much to do with the arrangement of the over-all work. The purpose of the book was to emphasize the "divine right" character of the primacy of the Holy See. In its review of the book, the *Living Church* said: "In the first place it is the veriest nonsense to reply [to the book] by charging disloyalty against the writers . . . we hasten to add that we have a large sympathy with these dreamers of iridescent dreams and a mirage does represent a far distant reality. The dreamers are the prophets of better things to come when men of other generations shall be able to realize what these could only dream of."

There was the nutshell of Father Paul's problem. He

was a dreamer of better days, and those of us who have lived long enough to see the tremendous rejuvenation of all the Churches brought about by the ecumenical movement are beginning to realize those hopes of Christian unity of which Father Paul and men like him could only dream. He was like a Moses who was allowed to see the Promised Land from afar but could not enter it.

Dreams are related to prayers. Both are intangible but while the former contemplates what might be, the latter confidently awaits the intervention of God in the affairs of men. When Spencer Jones suggested in 1907 that one day each year be set aside as a day of special prayer for Christian unity and public sermons on the pope, Father Paul immediately responded in the affirmative. Jones suggested St. Peter's feast day, June 29th, but Father Paul countered with the idea that eight days or an octave of prayer was necessary for such a tremendous work. He chose the time between the Feast of St. Peter's Chair in Rome (January 19th) and the Feast of the Conversion of St. Paul (January 25th). St. Peter represented the unchanging rock of faith in Christ which was the foundation of the Church, while St. Paul symbolized the dynamic extension of the Gospel to all nations. Father Paul chose as a prayer for this octave a text from the Roman Catholic liturgy then in use, a prayer the priest said before Holy Communion which prayed that God would grant to the Church "that peace and unity which are agreeable to Thy Will."

From the beginning of the Christian era all the great historic liturgies contained petitions for Christian unity. The *Didache* (A.D. 80) speaks of the many grains of wheat and the many grapes which come from all over the world to be changed into the one Body and Blood of Christ in the

Eucharist. This symbolizes the unity among Christians which is effected by the reception of Communion. The opening Great Litany of the Byzantine liturgy prays "for the peace of all the holy churches of God and for the union of them all." Anglicans in their Book of Common Prayer ask God "to inspire continually the universal Church with the spirit of truth, unity and concord."

It is doubtful, however, whether the ancient authors of these venerable liturgical prayers ever fully envisioned a situation like ours where the people of the New Covenant are divided into various distinct denominations and Churches. On the contrary, the text of the Mass for Christian Unity, which is now officially designated as the liturgy to be used by Roman Catholics when praying for Christian unity, was originally known as the Votive Mass for the Removal of Schism, and was instituted at the time of the Great Western Schism when there were three claimants for the papal throne. At that time, the question was not a divergence of doctrine but a dispute concerning the rightful occupant of the office of pope. Many older prayers had as the object of their petition the perfection of the bonds which already united the various members of the Church, such as faith, hope, and charity.

In addition to the official worship of the various Christian Churches, there have been in recent times a number of movements which sought to unite members of various confessions in a common effort to promote prayer for the unity of all Christians.

In the early 19th century several prayer campaigns, promoted by evangelical Protestants and associated with the great revivals of the period, called upon God to send forth the Holy Spirit upon all Christians. Even though these prayer movements transcended denominational lines, they usually did not contain specific reference to the visible unity of Christians as we now think of it, because the evangelicals were not so much concerned with the Church as a visible society. Their goal was to bring together Christians of various Churches to pray for renewal in the Holy Spirit.

The initiative for explicit prayer for Christian reunion came principally from Anglicans and from individual Roman Catholics.

In 1840, Father Ignatius Spencer, until recently an Anglican and now a Roman Catholic, met Newman and Pusey while visiting Oxford, and suggested to them that they start a Union of Prayer for Unity. Pusey had recently declined a similar invitation from the evangelicals (perhaps he was chary of the evangelical approach) and saw difficulties for the project. Newman did issue a Plan of Prayer for Union which was designed to be an effort by Anglicans alone to pray for unity, but the bishops gave little or no encouragement and the project ended there. Spencer's, however, was the first of many initiatives along these lines.

The first society formed with the explicit aim of unity was the Association for the Promotion of the Unity of Christendom. It was the result of efforts by Anglicans and Catholics. Founded in 1857 by Dr. Frederick George Lee, an Anglican; and Ambrose Philips de Lisle, a Catholic layman; the association claimed a membership of 5,000 Anglicans, 1,000 Catholics, and 300 Greek Orthodox by 1864. It published the *Union Review*, a periodical providing a variety of opinions and proposals for unity. Catholic participation was short-lived. On the petition of the Catholic hierarchy of England, the association was condemned in a harsh manner by the Holy Office in 1864. Anglican members who protested the condemnation were informed that prayer for unity under heretical auspices was impossible for Roman Catholics. Furthermore, the Holy Office pointed out that even though the association encouraged its members to be loyal to their own Churches, its support in the *Union Review* of the branch theory of the Church prohibited the participation of Catholics. Only the Roman Catholic Church, the Holy Office contended, could call itself Catholic.

Despite the Holy See's opposition to Catholic participation in the Association for the Promotion of the Unity of Christendom it did encourage prayer on the part of Catholics for the return of "dissidents" to the Roman Catholic Church. Pope Leo XIII suggested the use of the Rosary for this intention in 1895, and two years later asked that a novena of prayer be observed throughout the Roman Catholic world before the Feast of Pentecost for a reunion of Christian forces under the one shepherd, the pope.

The Lambeth Conferences, meeting at stated periods in London, regularly called upon all its Anglican participants to pray for the reunion of all Christians according to the will of Christ. Various times, such as the Tuesday before Ascension Day (1878), or the Feast of Whitsunday (1906) were suggested.

Father Paul and Spencer Jones envisioned a week of prayer which would pray explicitly for the "return" of non-Catholic Christians to the Holy See and the conversion of all peoples in the mission fields. In the pages of *The Lamp* Father Paul spread the idea of the octave, first called the Church Unity Octave and later named the Chair of Unity Octave to emphasize its papal orientation. Each of the eight days had its own intention: the return of "other sheep," the return of oriental separatists, the submission of Anglicans, that Lutherans and Continental Protestants find their way back to Holy Church, that Christians in America become one in union with the Chair of St. Peter, the return to the sacraments of lapsed Catholics, the conversion of the Jews, and the missionary conquest of the world.

In this form the octave was of interest only to pro-Roman Anglicans and Roman Catholics, but as we shall see, its evolution over the years made it the major force for continuing ecumenical sensitivity in the Churches in this century. It is understandable that Roman Catholics were favorably impressed. Cardinal O'Connell of Boston was one of its early supporters.

The octave helped to bring Father Paul to the attention of a larger number of prominent Roman Catholics just as his influence among Anglicans declined. And it was another small gesture of piety which brought the Society of the Atonement to the attention of the Roman See itself.

Although the little community at Graymoor was very poor, beginning in the year of 1901 one cent out of every dollar the friars and sisters received in alms was set aside for the pope. Twice each year the community observed the ancient custom of the medieval Church and sent this offering, called Peter's Pence, to Rome on the Feast of St. Peter's Chair in Rome (January 18—beginning of the Octave) and on the Feast of St. Peter in Chains (August 1st). Without fail they were courteously acknowledged by Pope Pius X through his Secretary of State, Cardinal Merry del Val. The first letter in the archives of the society thanked the community for the contribution of $10. Later that year the cardinal wrote that the Holy Father "is deeply touched by the act of generosity," and expressed the hope that everyone at Graymoor would be led "to the faith in the one true fold."

The two founders of Graymoor now faced the difficult question before them: should they seek admission to the Roman Catholic Church?

V

Linked Up to the
Great Dynamo of Rome

THE FINAL ANSWER to the perplexing dilemma of Father
Paul and Mother Lurana was forthcoming in 1909, one year
before the great World Missionary Conference at Edinburgh, Scotland, gave birth to the modern ecumenical
movement among Protestant and Orthodox Churches. In
the early part of 1909, Father Paul visited Monsignor C.G.
O'Keeffe, pastor of the Roman parish at Highland Falls,
across the river from Graymoor, in an effort to resolve his
growing confusion about the validity of Anglican orders.
That visit with O'Keeffe was inconclusive, however, and
Father Paul became even more depressed. Concern for him
led Mother Lurana to go to New York and seek an inter-

view with the Roman Catholic archbishop, John Farley. The archbishop advised her that a corporate reception of the society was for the moment impossible and suggested an individual reception once the society had been dissolved. On hearing this bad news, Father Paul decided to make an appointment with James Cardinal Gibbons of Baltimore, the leading ecclesiastic of the Roman Church in the United States. The meeting with the cardinal was set for Friday, March 5th, 1909.

Arriving at the cathedral in Baltimore, Paul found the cardinal vested in the sacristy and preparing for a solemn liturgy. Thus he was available for only a few minutes of conversation. After quickly revealing his desires, the founder was dismissed by the prelate with the words: "You are in good faith. Be patient and follow the leading and guidance of the Holy Spirit." Discouraged, Father Paul returned to the office of Gibbons's secretary who proposed that he might possibly contact the Apostolic Delegate to the United States, Monsignor Diomede Falconio. Falconio was both an avid reader of *The Lamp* and a Franciscan as well. Perhaps through him, Gibbons's secretary suggested, there would be an avenue for dispelling Paul's difficulties. Upon inquiry at the Apostolic Delegation in Washington, D.C., Father Paul found that no consultation would be feasible until sometime in August since Falconio was on his way to Rome. So a tentative meeting was arranged for early August 1909.

Assured of a favorable reception by the Apostolic Delegate, Father Paul was somewhat dismayed when the new Episcopal Bishop of Delaware, Frederick Joseph Kinsman, instructed him by letter to appear at the bishop's home in Wilmington with a full report on the affairs of the society. As the episcopal visitor of the society, Kinsman had, of course, every right to demand an accounting. During his conference with Kinsman, Graymoor's founder frankly discussed his personal difficulties about Anglican orders as well as his stand concerning the Roman See, papal primacy, and corporate reunion. Father Paul told the bishop he believed that Anglican orders were valid even though Rome had stated that they were not. Yet he also was sure "that the Catholic Faith is the faith as now defined by the Roman See." Naturally the bishop had some trouble understanding the logic of Father Paul's stance and could not reconcile what seemed to him to be outright contradictions. At the end of their meeting Bishop Kinsman promised his prayerful consideration and as early a decision as possible.

On July 5th, 1909, Father Paul had in hand a letter from Bishop Kinsman which first outlined the founder's position as presented previously in their conversation, and then declared that such a stance seemed to "resolve itself into the single proposition that you accept the whole teaching of the Roman Church save the single detail of the repudiation of Anglican Orders." "I must repeat," continued Kinsman, "that this proposition is an impossible one for a clergyman of our Church. My advice is that, in the interest of single-minded honesty and devotion to duty, you make the choice between the two Churches. You cannot serve either the Papal Church or the Protestant Episcopal Church well if you try to serve both at the same time." There was no doubt in his mind, said the bishop, that Father Paul should "give up Anglican Orders, make an unqualified submission to the Latin Church, and be a good Roman Catholic." Perhaps, at least subconsciously, Kinsman was stating his own dilemma, for a few years later he followed his own advice and joined the Roman Church.

Now Father Paul had what he had wanted for so long.

In Bishop Kinsman's letter, he was persuaded, was convincing evidence of the will of the Holy Spirit for himself and the society. Thus, on August 13th, 1909, he appeared before the Apostolic Delegate in Washington, D.C., to explain and plead his cause. After lengthy discussion, Monsignor Falconio directed Father Paul to compose a letter to the Apostolic Delegate in which the desired petitions to the Holy See were to be outlined. In turn, Falconio said he would forward the letter to Rome. By his letter of August 19th to Falconio, Father Paul thus petitioned the pope for a corporate reception of the society into the Roman Church and asked for papal "sanction, protection and governance, in order that the name and institute [Society of the Atonement], which we believe we have derived from Our Lord Jesus Christ, may be confirmed to us by His Vicar."

As the days passed into September 1909 without any answer from Rome, the founders and members of the society became increasingly anxious. One day Father Paul asked the foundress: "Well, Mother, when do you think the answer from Rome will come?" Mother Lurana replied: "Why, it will come on St. Francis's Day, October 4th, of course." Paul suggested Covenant Day, October 7th, might be more auspicious, "a further manifestation of God's love for the Society of the Atonement" and "another seal upon the Covenant He made with us."

In this instance male bravado triumphed over female intuition because October 4th passed uneventfully. But on the morning of October 7th, 1909, Father Paul trudged up the hill to the convent from the mailbox with a long envelope postmarked Washington, D.C. It was from the office of the Apostolic Delegate. Opening the letter, the founder informed the tiny assembled community "that His Holiness is much gratified to learn of your resolution and that of your Community, and that he hopes and prays for the happy outcome of your good dispositions." More important, the letter continued, "with regard to your Community there will be no objection to its continuing in the same way, even after its union with the Catholic Church," provided that it "conform to the rules laid down for such proceedings by Canon Law." In the future, the letter advised, "when the Community shall have given proof of its utility, steps may be taken to have it approved by the Holy See—provided everything proceeds regularly and successfully." On that ambiguous note, Rome had allowed the unprecedented to occur. What motivated Rome to allow this first corporate reception into the Church since the Reformation is today unknown.

Though Rome had, to be sure, allowed an entire non-Roman religious community to enter the Church, Vatican officials thereby gave absolutely no guarantee that the society would remain together after the reception. The community would have to comply fully with all the detailed canonical requirements concerning religious institutes and would be under the direct control of the diocesan bishops wherever there were friaries and convents of the society. Until the community really proved that it was stable and vital, there would always be the possibility that it could cease to exist through suppression, and the individual members would have to go their separate ways. While the answer from Rome must have seemed splendid to Father Paul and the others, there probably was not a full awareness in their minds of the real risk involved. As a society they could be there today and gone tomorrow should higher ecclesiastical officials so decide. It was as simple as that.

A few days later Father Paul, Archbishop Farley, and Monsignor Falconio met in New York City, and preparations began for the reception of the society. The details, including the delegation of Monsignor Joseph Henry Conroy to act in the archbishop's stead at the ceremony, were carefully worked out. Conroy was the vicar general of the far-flung diocese of Ogdensburg, New York, and a close friend of Father Paul. In a telegram to Conroy, Paul asked him to come to Graymoor for the Reception Day, October 30th, 1909. Unknown to the founder, Monsignor Conroy was already on his way.

On the morning of October 21st, 1909, as Conroy was going about his rounds of parish visitations near the border of Canada, he received a telegram from his secretary at the chancery in Ogdensburg. The telegram summarized an earlier letter from Father Paul in which the founder announced that the Society of the Atonement would probably soon be received corporately into the Roman Church and that, therefore, Conroy's assistance was requested. Realizing that a good deal of time had elapsed since Father Paul had sent his letter, Conroy decided to make immediate preparations for the long and arduous journey southward through the Hudson Valley to Graymoor. The corporate reception of the society would, Conroy knew, be a truly momentous historical occasion, the first such occurrence since the Reformation, and Conroy was determined to share the event at all costs.

More than four continuous days and nights of travel passed before Conroy stood at the front door of St. Francis's Convent to be greeted by Mother Lurana. To Conroy's surprise and joy, he discovered that he had been delegated by Archbishop Farley to represent the prelate at the reception ceremony on October 30th. It was already October 25th. Mother Lurana exclaimed in her diary that day: "What an answer to prayer and what a relief! Surely now everything will go right." The Mother's expectation proved to be quite unfounded. The same day that Monsignor Conroy arrived, Monsignor C.G. O'Keeffe from Highland Falls came to the convent to continue the instructions he had been providing for the members of the society prior to their reception. Given to the sartorial elegance common to domestic prelates of His Holiness in those days, O'Keeffe's attitude toward his unique assignment was excelled in boorishness only by the splender of his satin cassock with red piping and buttons, white slippers, and red stockings.

While Father Paul and Monsignor Conroy were conversing outside in the convent garden, O'Keeffe proceeded to interview each sister to ascertain the nature of her belief about Anglican orders. According to Mother Lurana's own account, when she entered the parlor, O'Keeffe's first words were: "Close that window!" which the foundress promptly did. "Now," he stated, "I want you to sign a declaration saying that you believe Anglican orders to be invalid." Catching her breath, Mother Lurana asked if she could discuss the matter further with Father Paul and Monsignor Conroy in the garden. But O'Keeffe was not to be put off and told her to write out the declaration in his presence first before she left the room.

In what was probably one of the most traumatic experiences of her life, Mother Lurana penned these words: "I accept the Church's ruling regarding Anglican orders and desire to bow my individual judgment to that decree." O'Keeffe was thus outfoxed by Lurana because her statement was a clever mix both of public submission and of private dissent. Having received the approval of the two clerics outside, Mother Lurana returned to the parlor and presented the document to O'Keeffe who commanded: "Sign it!" The monsignor was apparently proceeding with extreme caution. In fact he even advised Conroy that the instructions should be prolonged beyond the date set by the archbishop for the reception of the society. However, Conroy finally prevailed upon O'Keeffe to change his mind and follow the instructions of Archbishop Farley.

O'Keeffe's behavior and the arrival of Monsignor Conroy were not the only events that made October 25th, 1909, so memorable for members of the society. That morning, before the arrival of the two monsignors, Father Paul had vested himself in full liturgical garb, marched solemnly down the aisle of the convent chapel of Our Lady of the Angels, consumed the eucharistic hosts in the tabernacle and brought to a symbolic end one phase of the society's liturgical life.

We cannot be sure what went through Father Paul's mind as he emptied that tabernacle in the dark little chapel. But he certainly must have had questions as he did so. What were these white "Anglican" wafers, mere bread without significance? The Roman Church said so. Had he not been ordained to the presbyterate of the Church many years ago to bring the eucharistic presence of Jesus among those he served? The Roman Church said he was no priest and had no such power. Think of all those hours of devotion and adoration before that tabernacle. Was it all useless and in vain? The Roman Church said it was. Indeed there even seemed to be some doubt on the part of the Roman Church whether he was a baptized Christian. He and the

others, with the exception of Mother Lurana and some of
the children at Graymoor, had to be baptized again according to the ritual of the Roman Church. By then, no further
insult could be given, so Father Paul meekly submitted to
the provisions set forth by the ecclesiastical authorities.
Mother Lurana would only submit to having the Roman
ceremonies supplied later in private without actual rebaptism.

Perhaps it is just as well that we do not know what
was in Father Paul's mind and heart as he turned from the
tabernacle toward Mother Lurana. Upon extinguishing the
sanctuary lamp, Mother Lurana prayed: "God grant that
we do not have to wait too long for the red lamp's re-light-
ing." It was a mere five days before the red lamp glowed
again. But it truly must have been an excruciating experience for this group of deeply religious people, accustomed
as they were to daily eucharistic reception, to be deprived
of it. Thus, October 25th, 1909, was quite an arduous day
for the Society of the Atonement, but at least the worst
seemed to be over.

When Monsignor Conroy returned from a visit to
Archbishop Farley on October 26th, he brought with him
permission to celebrate the liturgy and reserve the Sacrament on Saturday, October 30th, 1909, the day of reception. To commemorate the event, the archbishop and his
secretary provided a chalice, missal, altar linens, and vestments. After the celebration of the Eucharist on Saturday
morning, October 30th, 17 Christians, including two friars,
five sisters, six tertiaries, and four children, were admitted
to the Roman Church at the hands of Monsignor Conroy.
"Thank God," Mother Lurana wrote that evening, "we are
safe in Saint Peter's Boat!" Safe, yes. But secure, no.

With a full-page spread entitled "The Convent That Changed Its Faith," *The New York Times* in its November 14th issue declared that "the action of this handful of men [*sic*], widely known for their lives of self-sacrifice to their cause, has come as a thunderbolt upon Protestant denominations. Without a doubt the consequences of the controversy thus aroused will be far-reaching." Indeed, the paper predicted, there would certainly be a "storm of criticism and indignation and even ridicule" as the result of "so unprecedented a departure." There were, of course, the expected congratulatory letters from Roman clergy and laity as well as from some Anglicans who held views similar to those of the founders but who chose instead to remain in their own Church. Other Anglican readers of *The Lamp*, while not approving the decision to join the Roman Church, were particularly concerned about the future of the magazine. Wrote one of these: "Surely, with a little readjustment, *The Lamp* can be carried with you across the spiritual river and set up, with much of the old attractiveness. . . . I vehemently hope so." Still others, with equal vehemence, condemned the society as a band of traitors to the cause of reunion. There was a storm brewing.

Two weeks after the reception of the society, a letter appeared in the leading Episcopal magazine, *The Living Church*. Written by the rector of the Church of the Advent, Boston, Massachusetts, and titled "The Seceding Community at Graymoor," the letter accused Father Paul of raising money and holding property under the guise of being a loyal Episcopalian while in reality he was a crypto-Roman. The author, the Reverend William Van Allan, maintained that consequently "an interesting moral question arises in connection with the secession of the Reverend

Lewis T. Wattson [Father Paul James Francis] and his immediate followers to the Roman Obedience." Did the property of the society belong to it any longer or should it instead revert to the Episcopal Church, now that the society had become Roman?

In succeeding issues of *The Living Church* a debate, at times intense and ugly, ranged between Father Paul and some of the magazine's Anglican correspondents. The discussion, if such it can be called, was curtailed, though not ended definitively, when finally there appeared a letter from the Reverend J. A. M. Richey, a professor at Nashotah House in Wisconsin, an influential and mainly high church Episcopal seminary. Father Richey had long been one of Father Paul's strongest opponents, even going to the extent of tearing up copies of *The Lamp* in front of the students and publicly denouncing the magazine as lighted by the fires of hell. When Richey suddenly came to the defense of Father Paul out of, as he said, "a spirit of broadmindedness as well as that of simple justice and fairness," this was an impelling sign to the readers and editors of *The Living Church* that the controversy should be brought to a conclusion. After a few parting shots, the magazine eventually was forced to print at the bottom of its correspondence column: "The discussion of this subject is now at an end." However excellent an editorial judgment that statement may have been, it was hardly indicative of what the future reality would be.

Also during November 1909, two good friends of Graymoor came to pay their respects to the members of the society. Around the middle of the month, Archbishop John Farley and Father Paschal Robinson, O.F.M., showed their concern for the tiny struggling community. The

Franciscan Father Paschal, who later became papal nuncio to Ireland and an archbishop, invested two friars and five sisters in the scapular and cord of the Third Order of St. Francis after the archbishop had confirmed the group earlier in the day. As he left the convent, Archbishop Farley announced that Father Paul was to begin studies for the Roman priesthood at once by entering St. Joseph's Seminary, Dunwoodie, New York. Because he would be needed to carry on the administration of the society, Father Paul was required to spend only four days a week at the seminary and could return to Graymoor every Thursday afternoon.

While he was at Graymoor Father Paul could not celebrate any of the liturgical ceremonies to which he had been accustomed as an Anglican clergyman. No doubt this was an extremely painful experience for him and for the community of sisters whose chaplain he had been for over ten years. Agonizing, because he knew that though he would be ordained a Roman priest after completion of studies, there would be absolutely no external difference in the kinds or outward forms of ecclesiastical functions he could perform. While he was an Anglican, he had firmly believed in his priestly orders and celebrated all the liturgical rites according to the usages of the Anglican high church party. In the liturgy, with the exception of the use of the vernacular and of the revised and adapted Book of Common Prayer, Father Paul could hardly be distinguished from his Roman counterparts. Today even those exceptions would scarcely be telling marks. How ironic it was, then, that Father Paul became almost powerless to work for Christian unity when he entered the Roman Church while he had had nearly unlimited freedom to do so as an Anglican clergyman.

Many years after his reception into the Roman Church, Father Paul still maintained that he was Catholic while an Anglican. In 1929 he remarked that "from the very beginning of this Institute its Founders were not Protestant; they believed in the Catholic Religion, loved the Catholic Church, understood what the Catholic Church was, and they had a special loyalty and devotion to the Vicar of Christ. . . ." Today there is no extant evidence that he ever denied or revised that statement. It seems that it was quite clear in the minds of Father Paul and Mother Lurana that they were always Catholic as members of the Anglican Church.

Since Father Paul could no longer act as chaplain to the sisters, both because he was considered a layman by the Roman Church and because of his four-day-a-week absence from Graymoor, the community of sisters found it had to rely on outsiders for spiritual services. Although the Archbishop of New York persisted in appointing chaplains of various kinds, one by one they came and rapidly went. As Mother Lurana put it in her diary, "the poor archbishop must think Graymoor a howling wilderness where no living priest can exist." She was far from incorrect when one considers the extremely primitive conditions there, the loneliness, the rugged climate, and the lack of the amenities which most diocesan priests expected as a part of their assignment in those days. Though Graymoor was a mere 50 miles north of New York City, that area of Putnam County was sparsely populated, and the only major highway, the Albany Post Road, was narrow and dirt constructed. Graymoor was a half mile from the Post Road through dense forests and hills. Because of their difficulty in retaining chaplains, therefore, the sisters were frequently deprived of the liturgy for five and six days at a stretch.

Even when Father Paul was present, nothing could happen if no Roman priest were available. So it became more and more urgent that the founder receive the proper credentials in order to resume his position as chaplain.

On the day after Archbishop Farley confirmed the small band at Graymoor in November, 1909, therefore, Father Paul obediently set off for Dunwoodie to begin his studies. And what a sight he was. Not wearing his familiar gray-brown habit, but dressed in a black suit donated by the archbishop, he bade farewell to the sisters. Lamented Mother Lurana: "It was dreadful to see him out of the dear gray-brown habit. One of the sisters cried." Because the foundress had been largely responsible for the design and color of the habit, perhaps she had a slightly exaggerated view of its importance. Yet it is ironic that the first time Father Paul had not worn his habit in public since the day he was clothed in it was as a Roman Catholic layman. In the eyes of the Roman Church he was, of course, stripped of orders and of vows.

At the seminary, by command of the archbishop, Paul was addressed as "Brother," a title which, though no doubt well-intended, must also have been hard for him to accept after having heard "Father" for the nearly 25 years since the day of his Anglican ordination. In general, however, he was cordially received at the seminary by students and professors alike. Because of his unusual situation and background, the only examination required of him was an oral one at year's end, and he was never called on for class participation. How excruciating this situation must have been for one of the finest preachers of the Episcopal Church and one of the brightest students in his class at the General Theological Seminary. Yet "Brother" Paul kept up the routine of four days at Dunwoodie and three days at Gray-moor for almost nine months, no mean accomplishment in view of the huge amount of correspondence that awaited him on his desk every Thursday afternoon, the necessity of publishing *The Lamp* each month without fail, and the increasing pressures of internal community affairs.

How frustrated, then, Father Paul must have been when the rector of the seminary informed him at the end of the scholastic year that although he would receive the orders of subdeacon and deacon, there was no possibility of ordination as priest until some time in 1911, a year hence. "Linked up to the great dynamo of Rome," his own words, he often found that he was short-circuited by people and events in the Roman Church. Under the date of June 8th, 1910, however, Mother Lurana wrote in her diary: "A letter from Father Paul tells us the wonderful news that Archbishop Farley will ordain him on June 16th, in the Seminary chapel." Evidently something had changed the archbishop's mind.

In Mother Lurana's opinion, the reversal was due to a novena made in honor of Our Lady of Perpetual Help whose feast at that time was celebrated on June 16th. More probably, the actual reasons were the archbishop's continuing failure to obtain a permanent chaplain for the sisters, Father Paul's impressive theological competence which he had demonstrated in the year's end examinations, and, as we shall see, the inauguration in March 1910 of a property lawsuit against the sisters, something that the archbishop knew would put great demands on the time and energies of the founder. Whatever the case, on June 16th, 1910, Paul regained the right to use "Father" once more, this time in the Roman Church.

At the ceremony of ordination there were only a few close friends including Mother Lurana. She recorded that evening: "I cannot describe the wonderful ceremony any more than I can describe the dignity of our Father, nor the look upon his face. A true son of St. Francis in his gray-brown habit and white vestments and white linen alb, embroidered in blue with Our Lady's monogram and lilies. Ah, now, no one can question his priesthood, a priest forever, forever." In the absence of contrary evidence, it might be suggested that just as the founders had no doubt after their reception into the Roman Church about their catholicity while still Anglicans, so also they were quite certain that Father Paul had been a validly ordained priest of the Catholic, though not Roman, Church. The evidence in this regard is both inferential and circumstantial to be sure, but a case can be made for maintaining that Father Paul and Mother Lurana privately believed that Anglican orders were valid even after their reception into the Roman Church.

As has been noted, Father Paul celebrated his last Anglican liturgy only five days before reception into the Roman Church. At the end of that liturgy he opened the tabernacle and consumed the hosts while Mother Lurana extinguished the sanctuary lamp exactly as any Roman priest and sister would have done when a Roman chapel was closed or to be unused for some time. From that moment on, Mother Lurana refused to enter the chapel until the day of reception. Evidently, in her mind, something was missing in that chapel which had been very much present there before. Her stated wish that the very same sanctuary lamp would soon be relighted for its intended purpose—to signal the Presence of Christ in the Eucharist —points in a similar direction.

Quoting a lecture of Father Robert Hugh Benson, noted English author, after Benson's reception into the Roman Church from Anglicanism, Father Paul, in a 1907 issue of *The Lamp*, pleaded for understanding of Benson's action by using these words from the lecture: "At that time I believed that we had a true priesthood, and we practiced Catholic doctrine. We had what we believed to be the Mass. . . . I cannot bear those people who say that the Angelican Church is a mockery. It is not true, and to call it a mockery is almost as much as to say that its clergy were playing a hypocritical part. We were not. We believed that we were true priests. . . . " What Father Paul quoted from Benson in 1907, he could just as well, it seems, have repeated in June 1910 after his ordination to the Roman priesthood. From that date on, indeed, his priesthood could not be questioned. What can still be queried today is whether the founders personally ever did deny the validity of Anglican orders after they became members of the Roman Church.

In the public arena, of course, they were compelled to abide by the teaching of the Roman Church and the decision of Leo XIII condemning Anglican orders. No one in as vulnerable a position as the founders would dare to state the contrary in public, especially when it is remembered that those were the days of the Modernist controversy under Pope Pius X, when the slightest doctrinal divergence was cause for suspicion and even ecclesiastical censure. With regard to their private thoughts and beliefs about the validity of Anglican orders, however, the matter will be clouded in uncertainty and ambiguity until very weighty evidence one way or the other is forthcoming.

Upon his ordination, Father Paul was faced with yet another controversy. During March 1910, the New York City law firm of Zabriskie, Murray, Sage and Kerr began action for their clients, Dr. Arthur Lowndes and co-trustees, to gain title to the small plot of land at Graymoor on which stood St. John's Church and St. Francis's Convent. Because no deed had been drawn and properly registered to transfer the property to the Sisters of the Atonement from the three original owners, Mrs. Sally Nicholson, Miss Julia Chadwick, and Miss Alice Elliot, the community of sisters had hardly a legal leg on which to stand. It was clear to Father Paul that there was a very real possibility that the trustees would win any action in court and the sisters would be evicted from convent and church. Such an outcome was unthinkable, at least for Father Paul, who spent many hours trudging from one law firm to another in hope of finding a way out of their dilemma. Not so Mother Lurana.

In a letter dated January 26th, 1911, and addressed to the lawyers for the plaintiffs, Lurana announced that she was "permitting the case to go by default," but that the reason for doing so, she said, was "not because I am indifferent to the very painful consequences that will result to us, or because I do not believe in the validity and equity of our right to remain in possession of this property, and our ability to prove the justice of our claim in the courts." From the viewpoint of human prudence Mother Lurana's given reasons for not fighting the case in court are amazing—and admirable.

First, she remarked, "we are Franciscans, and our holy Founder, St. Francis of Assisi . . . told his first children in the Order that they should *not offer resistance*. . . ." Second, Lurana continued, "the special work of the Society of the Atonement is Church Unity, . . . and I would rather that our little band of Sisters were homeless than that we be the means of a legal battle that could not help but stir up uncharity and strife between the Catholic Church and Anglicans. . . ." Admitting that such a position might seem "very academic," even "fanatical," the foundress revealed that she personally had a "very real temptation to fight it out" but that she did not dare do so "on conscientious grounds." Third, the Mother added, "it is our earnest hope that your clients, having achieved a legal victory and having had this, our home, handed over to them, will then meet us in some reasonable financial settlement." There then followed in the letter her draft of a legal brief of formidable proportions. At the end of her letter Lurana poignantly asked: "In a court of law does it not also count that a woman, relying upon the word and good faith of the Trustees, put her all in a little house on the land they promised to give her; that she and those with her worked faithfully to fulfill their trust, and just because they became Catholics are turned out of the little home built by themselves, the place over which they had been in control and of which they have borne all expenses for twelve years?" Of such stuff are valiant women made.

At that moment, however, one of the trustees, Miss Julia Chadwick, contested the petition of the plaintiffs on the ground that she had already faithfully discharged her duties as trustee and that the sisters had fully met the terms of their contract to minister to the spiritual needs of the people in the vicinity of Graymoor. As a result of Miss Chadwick's action, the law case dragged on for six more years until the November 1917 issue of *The Lamp* informed its readers that "Judge Tompkins of the Supreme Court of the State of New York had rendered judgment in favor of the plaintiffs in the suit which they began over seven years ago to dispossess the Sisters. . . ." Worse still, the plaintiffs would not consider any financial settlement at all, and the sisters thus had a mere 60 days in which to vacate the premises.

Legally, however, there was still the possibility of an appeal to the Appellate Court. Against such an action Mother Lurana remained adamant. She informed the sisters' lawyer that "we will not take our case to the Court of Appeals (unless the ecclesiastical authorities of this Catholic Archdiocese should insist)." Frustrated, the sisters' lawyer, Mr. James Dempsey, besought the foundress to change her mind. "As I personally emphasized to you," he wrote, "the advisability of an appeal is indispensable, as you have everything to gain thereby and practically nothing to lose." His plea went unheeded. Days went by, eating up precious time. The sisters began preparations for moving out of the convent and church. And then, in one of those fortuitous occurrences that change the course of history, Father Paul went to cast his vote on Election Day, November 8th, 1917, in nearby Garrison.

On the street Paul met Mr. Hamilton Fish, son of a former governor of New York State, and himself three times Speaker of the Assembly. Moreover, he was Senior Warden of St. Philip's Episcopal Church in Garrison and, most importantly, a member of the Standing Committee of the Episcopal Diocese of New York. In casual conversation Father Paul mentioned that the sisters were soon going to be evicted from their convent because they had lost their legal battle and would not appeal the decision. To Father Paul's delight, Mr. Fish, after expressing his strong disapproval of what had happened, immediately offered his professional services to the sisters. In no time he had drawn up and circulated among the townsfolk and parishioners of St.

Philip's Church a strong petition calling on Episcopal Bishop David Greer of New York, as well as George Zabriskie, attorney for the plaintiffs, and the trustees to cease and desist from evicting the sisters and to accept instead a settlement of $2000 for the property.

During a meeting of the trustees and counsel, which had been arranged by Bishop Greer, Mr. Fish and the bishop eventually persuaded the trustees to make a financial settlement with the sisters. Victory for the community appeared in sight. However, Mr. Fish apparently had over-looked the fact that George Zabriskie was not only an eminent lawyer but also the Chancellor of the Episcopal Diocese of New York. And Chancellor Zabriskie would hear nothing of any such settlement. Still Mr. Fish was not above pulling rank himself. Father Paul later described what happened at this apparent impasse: "Mr. Fish played the part of Portia, and to the consternation of Shylock declared that he would prepare and introduce a bill into the State Legislature making the transfer of the property lawful." To everyone's amazement Mr. Zabriskie at that time was dismissed as the lawyer for the plaintiffs.

On March 13th, 1918, the bill authorizing the transfer of the property to the sisters was introduced into the state legislature, passed the assembly quickly at Mr. Fish's urging; and was signed by the governor on March 21st. Little more than a month later, the Mother Foundress rejoiced that "the mail today brought *the letter* from the office of Judge O'Brien containing the good news we have been awaiting —the deed is signed by the Trustees. . . . Words fail at such a time. I can only say '*Deo Gratias*' to the Prince of Kings of the earth, He who can so mightily protect His own, His poor spouses."

A final irony must be recorded here. Through contact with the Sisters of the Atonement, all three of the plaintiffs in the law suit eventually entered the Roman Catholic Church, and two of them, Miss Elliot and Mrs. Nicholson, died at Graymoor and are buried in the sisters' cemetery there. When writing about the death of Miss Elliot many years after the lawsuit, Father Paul devoted a mere seven lines of a more than 1200-word eulogy of her to the facts of that unpleasant case. The whole affair, Paul said in *The Lamp*, occurred because the three plaintiffs had been "impelled by influences brought to bear and their own conscientious scruples. . . ." If nothing else, Father Paul was as generous as Mother Lurana was strong. There is no final glory without first suffering.

VI

The Rain Fell and Floods Came
but the House was Built
on a Rock

NOW THAT THE LITTLE COMMUNITY OF FRANCISCANS had settled the problem of their ecclesiastical allegiance, several pressing problems proposed themselves. The first was that of personnel. Although many came and went on brief visits to Graymoor, there were only two "permanent" friars on hand when the community entered the Roman Catholic Church in 1909, Father Paul and Brother Anthony. With the announcement of its Roman Catholic affiliation, the community began to attract young recruits from its new religious constituency. They were very young, as a matter of fact, mostly boys of high-school and college age needing an education. Because Father Paul knew that his ecumenical vision would not be realized unless the Children of the Atonement began to increase, he had long hoped for the establishment of a school in which young men could be trained to carry on the apostolate of the community. As we shall see in the following chapter, a donor providentially appeared, and it was with happy heart that Father Paul watched Auxiliary Bishop Cusack of New York break ground for St. John's minor seminary on May 21st, 1912. Little more than a year passed and the school opened on September 1913 with a grand total of four students.

With his usual expansive spirit Father Paul announced to readers of *The Lamp*: "We have four young men to start with, in the new House of Studies, and others will be coming soon, we trust, and these should have plenty of good milk to drink. It is time the Friars had a cow. Who will give us one for our lads?" He got the cow, in fact several of them, and an increasing number of students kept the bovines quite well occupied.

By 1914 there were two novices and seven scholastics, and Father Paul talked of enlarging the seminary building even though he knew the original house would be adequate for a long while at that rate of growth. In great hope and with perhaps a bit of imprudence he broke ground for a new addition in June 1914.

No sooner was the addition to the seminary completed than a near disaster occurred. Two years previously Father Paul had received into the community a Father Francis Bethel. Apparently the new recruit already had theological training because he was ordained to the priesthood in the fall of 1914. The Mother Foundress wrote in her diary: "It is such a benefit to the Community to have a Friar [priest] of our own Society. . . ." But the blessing turned out to be a curse. Some quirk in Francis' personality soon created an untenable situation.

Young and inexperienced, Father Francis found himself in rather unusual circumstances on the Mount of the Atonement in those early days. Because Father Paul was one of the most celebrated preachers along the Eastern seaboard, he was frequently absent from Graymoor on speaking engagements. Someone had to mind the store, and the mantel fell on Father Francis. Though intelligent, he was a terrible administrator, and he had delusions of grandeur. He looked forward to the day when Father Paul would be removed as superior and he could take the founder's place. With that ambition, Francis readily accepted stories that were being circulated at the time by Father Paul's detractors in the Roman Church. These persons, some clergy and some laity, felt that Father Paul was a hopeless visionary, that Graymoor was "too Protestant," and that the community would as a result soon be suppressed by the ecclesiastical authorities. Graymoor just would not last, they said.

Francis probably felt himself to be on the side of both the Church and the community. His solution was to get rid of Father Paul; only then would the society have a chance for survival. His method was vicious. He resented the close relationship between the two founders and pictured it as unseemly. Father Francis convinced himself that Mother Lurana's influence on Father Paul was far greater than it should be and had to cease.

During one of Father Paul's frequent absences in early March 1915, Father Francis and Brother Paschal, his close friend and another new member of the community, set in motion the events which they believed would bring control of the community into their hands and destroy the linger-

ing influence of Mother Lurana upon the affairs of the
society. For some months the two friars had been trying to
discredit Father Paul. They began with little things, like
taking the books and materials Father Paul needed in his
work on the rule and constitution of the society. Next they
tampered with his personal mail, an act incompetently done
since the founder became aware that someone was opening
and resealing his letters. In fact he told Mother Lurana as
much at the time, according to her diary. Brother Paschal
was the culprit here. He had also extended his operations
to the financial records of the community. But of this
Father Paul was unaware because Brother Paschal had the
only key to the friary safe. If Father Paul had been home
more, he would also have noticed that there was something
irregular about the class schedules of the handful of students in the small seminary that had been established at
Graymoor. Actually, for days on end there were no classes
held at all under the tutelage of Father Francis, who was
very busy about other matters.

Father Francis circulated rumors among the students
that Graymoor might soon be closed and that they had
better prepare to leave as quickly as possible. Indeed, he
promised that Brother Paschal would even pay their fares
back home. To the delight of Father Paul's enemies in the
Roman Church, Francis confirmed everything they believed was true about the founder. Father Paul, Francis
said, was a silly man with all sorts of strange visions and
was puffed up with extraordinary pride. Father Paul placed
too much confidence in Mother Lurana and was too intimate with her to be a good religious. Father Paul was a
bungler and was so inept he could not successfully run a
religious community. Father Paul was a crypto-Protestant

who was tainting the young minds of the students at Graymoor with heresy.

By early March 1915, Father Paul came to indisputable knowledge of what Francis and Paschal were up to. He could defer no longer. Intent on rectifying matters, he sought an immediate interview with Thomas F. Cusack, Auxiliary Bishop of New York, whom Cardinal Farley had appointed to oversee the fledgling community. To Father Paul's relief, Bishop Cusack advised him that Brother Paschal should be dismissed without delay before worse things happened. On hearing the news from Father Paul about his dismissal, Paschal refused to leave and told Paul that he had had a subsequent word from Bishop Cusack ordering him to remain until advised otherwise. Later that night after the friars had retired, Paschal sneaked out of the friary and walked the five miles to Peekskill where he telephoned Father Francis who was on his way to a retreat on the orders of Father Paul, who still hoped his spiritual son would repent of his deeds.

Next morning the two cohorts roared up the dirt road to Graymoor with taxi cabs and a truck. Loudly protesting that Brother Paschal was going to be dismissed, Father Francis kept the founder busy in the friary office while his partner was gathering the bewildered students and novices for a quick getaway. This last scenario was poignantly related by Father Paul who wrote that no one of the departing students was "allowed by the conspirators to say one word to me, not even goodbye."

However, Francis had plenty to say to the students as he wildly waved around a telegram that supposedly gave him authorization from Bishop Cusack to investigate affairs at the friary and to report to the prelate that very afternoon. Naturally, the students were impressed, and they followed orders without discussion. Only two students chose to remain with Father Paul. As one of the students who departed recalled later in a written statement, he and the others were victims of a "conspiracy which was made between Father Francis and Brother Pascal to injure Father Paul and if possible to ruin the community." It was done, the student maintained, "for revenge" when the two friars "realized their inability to 'control' the community." The former seminarian, called "T.M.", was amazed, he said, when on the way to the railroad station at Garrison, Brother Paschal remarked that "it would be a good thing to lay the state of affairs before the *Menace* and get a fortune of several thousand dollars out of the scandal." The *Menace*, a rabid, anti-Roman magazine in the worst tradition of yellow journalism, would have been more than happy to comply.

Fortunately, the ecclesiastical authorities in New York kept a very tight wrap on any information about the affair. At an interview with Bishop Cusack a few days later, Father Paul learned, first, that Father Francis had had no correspondence with the bishop, and, secondly, that Bishop Cusack had certainly not sent the telegram Francis had used to rout the students. Little by little the whole story of the plan to demean and destroy him became clear to Father Paul: "I have now learned that this attempt to ruin our Institute has been going on in secret for weeks." Commenting on the day when the two friars drove away with the students, Mother Lurana remarked: "I cannot write any more of this pitiful thing. My pity and my heart-ache is for the priest who, still wearing the habit of the Society, could do such a deed; come like a destroyer to tear down with his own hands what he, himself, had worked so hard to build up. Truly the devil is hard on his dupes."

Within days, however, who should appear in the office of the founder but Father Francis. Quite unrepentant and explaining away what had happened as a mere mistake, Francis pompously declared that he was ready to take up his duties again as before. But Father Paul had had enough of him by then. He was prompt to release Francis from his obligations to the society, gave him a letter of recommendation, and offered him some money with the promise of further financial assistance if needed. It was all done with civility and prayerfulness. Before Francis's final leave-taking the two prayed together in the chapel, not only that Francis would persevere in the Roman priesthood but that the society would grow and develop in its ecumenical mission. No departure from a religious community is easy, but it is the measure of Father Paul that he went to extraordinary lengths in this case to heal the rift caused by another's treachery.

The red sanctuary lamp cast a soft glow upon the two men as they met together in a small chapel atop the Mount of the Atonement. It was painful for Father Paul to kneel there beside his spiritual son in front of the Blessed Sacrament. But he knew what he must do and say. He turned to Father Francis Bethel and whispered: "I may forget to pray for you, others may forget to pray for you, but there is one whom you have deeply wronged and she will never forget to pray for you." That reference to Mother Lurana was the sad but prayerful end to a bizarre affair: a "putsch" that failed.

Not only did Father Paul discipline himself because of the near tragedy with Father Francis and Brother Paschal but he also had substantial reason to bring increased order into the affairs of his community. An outside certified accountant was employed. A rigorous schedule for the seminary was devised and enforced. Infractions by the members of the society were often severely punished, and Father Paul gained a reputation as a severe taskmaster. However undesirable many of these developments may seem, he had too much to lose otherwise, as had the Roman Church and the cause of unity. The tragedy also had an effect on Father Paul's health, for Mother Lurana wrote under date of June 1st, 1916: ". . . tomorrow Father will undergo his operation. It will, I think, be a serious one. It seems such a dreadful thing to strike down a man in apparently excellent health (for Father has slowly gotten back the ground he lost in the shock of a year and a half ago)."

Moreover, Father Paul's reputation had been severely damaged among the authorities of the Archdiocese of New York, Bishop Cusack, of course, had made a full report on the debacle with Father Francis and Brother Paschal to Archbishop Farley, and Father Paul was subsequently called to a meeting with archdiocesan officials. He learned from this encounter with the ecclesiastical authorities that law and order are essential elements in successfully governing a religious community whatever other deficiencies might possibly exist in it. He was quick to take the hint. Nonetheless, it would be many years before Graymoor recovered completely from this disaster. Even after his death the suspicions about the instability and financial insolvency of the community were not put to rest in the minds of some who were in position of higher ecclesiastical authority. Nor did criticisms of Father Paul and Graymoor abate among the lower clergy over the years.

Father Paul with his tonsured novices in St. Francis Chapel

Fifteen years after the attempt to destroy the society, there were a number of renewed attacks on the integrity of the founder. Surprisingly, one of these came in the pages of *The Acolyte*, today titled *The Priest*, a magazine widely distributed among Roman Catholic clergy in the United States. The other onslaught came in the far less well-known parish bulletin, *The Mentor*, issued by the Roman Catholic Church of the Nativity, Brooklyn, New York. The two complaints were, however, of a piece. Entitled "Out of the Mouth of Sucklings," the article in *The Acolyte* was a scurrilous attack on Father Paul and others whom the author called "promoters of shrines." Both the *Catholic News* of New York and the *Catholic Register* of Denver came under censure by *The Acolyte* for running advertisements of "shrines" which supposedly bilked poor parishes of money that was "sorely needed at home."

Further, the article satirically described Father Paul as "The Shepherd of Graymoor" who was busy fleecing the sheep of their coins in order to run Graymoor's activities in another pasture. Likening *The Lamp* to the British Empire, upon which the sun never sets, the article complained that not only did *The Lamp* promote all sorts of money-making schemes and false devotions, but it also advertised "for eighth-grade boys to enter the order. A rather tender age at which to decide a boy's vocation. . . . Granted also that money is sent for foreign missions and home needs, the main thing is a grand shrine which will serve to draw the thousands mentioned. . . ." The article went on with this work of destruction for several more pages.

Such charges are, however, easily and quickly dismissed in view of the facts. True, Father Paul was a creative master at fund-raising. A look at the records, however, shows that the community all too often lived from hand to mouth, while money was being disbursed to the poor and needy at home and abroad. Until Father Paul's death, Graymoor was a quaint and shabby collection of stuccoed buildings, Sears Roebuck hand-me-downs, and an ugly, unfinished "shrine" in honor of St. Anthony, which was the size of a small parish church. And whatever one might think today about the advisability of high-school seminaries, such schools were extremely common at the time these charges were made. Indeed, the minor seminaries were promoted and demanded by the very highest ecclesiastical authorities.

All this time Father Paul remained absolutely silent, perhaps feeling that his accusers were unworthy of his attention. Sometimes, however, he must have yearned for the good old Anglican days when a battle over substantive issues was in order. Besides, Father Paul had more than enough to keep him busy while his society grew and expanded during the two decades subsequent to the tragedy which nearly destroyed it in 1915.

His first real building project other than the friary had been undertaken as early as 1911. And the following year, Father Paul proudly watched the completion of Graymoor's Chapel of St. Francis. The small church was patterned after the Basilica of St. Francis in Assisi and constructed almost entirely by volunteer help. The *Pittsburgh Observer*, in reporting the dedication of the chapel, put it this way: "Tramps, just plain tramps, did a large part of the work of constructing the Chapel of St. Francis, which the Franciscan Friars in New York dedicated recently. Thousands of wayfarers have helped, and in the words of the Friars have proved themselves worthy disciples of

Christopher, the 'walking saint'." Needing an architect for the building, Father Paul obtained the services of Monsignor John Cyril Hawes, a former Anglican clergyman, whom the founder had received into the Roman Church. In appreciation for Father Paul's kindness to him, Hawes offered to design a chapel.

As an Anglican priest, Hawes had built six stone churches in the Bahamas, where he had labored for many years. Eventually ordained a Roman priest, Hawes continued his rather unique hobby both in Australia and, once again, in the Bahamas. Known as the "Hermit of Cat Island," Monsignor Hawes always considered his gift to Father Paul one of his finest architectural creations. Restored to its original beauty, the chapel today stands as one more testimony to the inspiration which Father Paul engendered in the thousands of persons whose lives he touched.

Near the St. Francis Chapel was an ugly chicken coop. To Father Paul, though, it looked something like the log cabin in which Abraham Lincoln was born. Thinking that the chickens could do without their little house better than the many "knights of the road" who visited Graymoor could go without proper shelter, Father Paul determined to move the hens out and the men in. Thus, from this humble beginning, the first St. Christopher's Inn was born. From the start there had been men coming to seek the hospitality of Graymoor, as the testimony of one lady reveals when she recounted her visit there in 1910: ". . . one of the things that touched me was the way they treat everyone to the same fare—there is no difference for tramps or us—and there are always tramps there, winter and summer—and they welcome them all and call them 'Brothers Christopher'."

Because he had a deep respect for human dignity, Father Paul was not about to call these men "tramps," no matter how down-and-out they might appear. Hence it was not with any paternalism or disdain that he called them "Christophers" or Christ-bearers. Rather, the appellation resulted from the deep seriousness with which Father Paul took the scriptural verses: "Come blessed of my Father . . . for I was hungry and you fed me; I was thirsty and you gave me drink; I was a stranger and you took me in; naked and you covered me; sick and you visited me. . . ." There was no intent on Father Paul's part to involve himself or his community in rehabilitative work with alcoholic males, at least with any high degree of professionalism. Instead Father Paul believed that a good night's sleep, a decent diet, proper clothing, medical assistance, and even spiritual help when requested could do as much for the unfortunate, distressed, and downtrodden as many a skilled professional. Father Paul demanded that every man have a place of respect in the human community at Graymoor. Every man should feel needed. No man should think he was a burden, an outcast, an inmate of some insensitive institution.

The Inn was an expression of Father Paul's great love for men and his deep desire that every man be reconciled —at-one—with himself, with society, and with God. Thus, there have never been any restrictions about the race, creed, or color of the men who are guests of the Inn. There are no fees. There is a minimum of rules and regulations. There are few personal questions asked. There is no red tape. The Inn still exists as a miracle of its own kind in our bureaucratic, technological, and complex world. It is not a hospital. It is not a home for senior citizens. It is not a resort. It is the love of Christ for men at work. It is a restatement of the Gospel in the 20th century, a protest against the excessive individualism of the self-made man, a call to public concern for the less fortunate. And from all walks of life these Christ-bearers come, saddled with problems—loss of a job, death of a spouse, a divorce, drug abuse, alcoholism—whatever it may be. Of all ages, of all religions or none, of all skin colors, of many nations, the Brothers Christopher form a mighty band of those who have had the courage and humility to say "help me." They are an army of witnesses against the proud and the powerful who see no merit in weakness or need.

Over the years the facilities of the Inn expanded and improved, thanks to the generosity of people who knew that "there but for the grace of God go I." Responding to one of many outraged readers of *The Lamp* who resented the fact that those they considered "hoboes" or "tramps" were called "Brother" and "Christopher," Father Paul summed up the reason for the Inn's existence when he wrote:

The zeal of our correspondent is of course to be commended insofar as he desires to protect the good name of those who bear the honored and sacred title of Brother in Holy Religion; but we maintain that these can suffer no more indignity by sharing the name of Brother with the least and humblest in the Kingdom of God, though he chance to be a vagabond, and a social outcast, or the poorest of beggars, than has the Son of God in stooping to take our humanity into union with His Godhead and to call these very same "Hoboes" if you will, *His* brothers.

At the same time another reader replied in turn: "We are all tramping onward to eternity. Some like Lazarus and others like Dives. Over nineteen hundred years ago Our Blessed Lady and St. Joseph had to tramp looking for shelter where the infant Jesus might be born. His coming has made us all brothers . . . brothers we are and brothers we will have to be." Love sometimes is contagious.

Father Paul's concern for the "down-and-out" was not confined only to Graymoor. When the village of Peekskill, New York, closed its municipal shelter for indigent men in order to rid the community of "undesirables," Father Paul wrote a strongly worded letter of protest to the chairman of the Board of Councilmen. Addressing Mr. Thomas Nelson, Jr., the founder attacked the council for perpetrating an un-American and un-Christian act.

It was un-American, said Father Paul, because the Declaration of Independence states that all men have certain inalienable rights given by the Creator and that among these are life, liberty, and the pursuit of happiness. Food and shelter, particularly in winter, are elements constituting both life and happiness. For the village of Peekskill to deny any man, however indigent, access to food and shelter is a violation of his rights as an American citizen. The action of the council was un-Christian, he maintained, because Jesus made identification with the poor a determining factor in a person's eternal future. Such indigent persons are no menace to the community, if treated properly. On the contrary, he said, "if you treat them inhumanly and contrary to the law of Christ, they will indeed prove a menace and a danger by bringing down Divine chastisement upon the town."

Most of these men, Father Paul continued, offer to work for what they receive. But even if they did not work, the obligation to help them would still exist:

Even if it were true [that some prefer to live off others than do an honest day's work], it does not either in the eyes of God or of the Commonwealth relieve Peekskill or any other village, town or city of our Republic from the poor man's burden. He is a constituent element in human society and must be humanely dealt with. We are bound by the law of our common brotherhood to shoulder the burden of supporting the helpless and indigent in a way which will most subserve the interests of all concerned.

Drawing his argument to a close, Father Paul asked the fathers of Peekskill if the village did not owe these men, disabled by alcoholism, some recompense because the town's streets were lined with saloons where they drank and a major industry in the village was the manufacture of brewing yeast used to make the very alcohol they consumed. There must have been some uncomfortable squirming at the next council meeting when Paul's letter was read.

A few years after the chicken coop became St. Christopher's Inn, the near disaster with Father Francis and Brother Paschal nearly emptied the newly founded St. John's Seminary. That was only a momentary set-back, however. Over the span of nearly 40 years the seminary educated several thousand young men, some of whom became priests and brothers in the society. Therein lay another problem.

What was to be done with those young men who had completed their training at St. John's seminary and at the novitiate? Where would they go to complete their education for the priesthood? There was not really an immediate problem, however, until the early 1920s when burgeoning numbers demanded a better arrangement than assigning one or two men to reside at seminaries run by the diocesan clergy or other religious communities. With such a situation existing, it was almost impossible to form young clerics in the tradition and spirit of the community. As had been the case many times before, a providential solution was forthcoming.

In 1922 a large tract of land, more than 30 acres, near the Catholic University of America in Washington, D.C., went on the market for sale. Known as the "Robinson property," the acreage was mostly wooded and was situated on a hill overlooking the university. A large brick mansion, a caretaker's cottage, and a stable comprised the only buildings on that rather sizable tract. Ever since the founding of the university, religious communities had been buying land in the environs and building houses of study where young men could reside while attending the university and preparing for ordination to the priesthood. By 1920 there was precious little land available for purchase except the Robinson property, which was the choicest of all.

With almost no money and very few students on hand, Father Paul made a momentous decision for the future of the society. He would buy that land. After many long months of negotiation and fund-raising, the estate finally became the property of the community during the early spring of 1923. Announcing the establishment of the Atonement Seminary of the Holy Ghost, Father Paul remarked in *The Lamp*: "Only time can tell what educational buildings will be erected on these thirty-three precious acres, and what enormous influence they will exert in the future worldwide expansion of our Holy Society."

At that time the founder had not yet fully paid the debt on the property, and his entire community consisted of only four priests, five clerics, and twenty minor seminarians. If nothing else, Father Paul was an optimist. He was also quite correct in his vision. Not only have several generations of friars become alumni of Atonement semi-nary, but today on that original tract also stand the Washington Retreat House for Women, which is run by the Sisters of the Atonement; St. Josaphat's Eastern Rite Seminary; Archbishop Carroll High School for Boys; St. Joseph's Carmelite Priory; and a new Atonement seminary, the old Robinson mansion having been demolished after many years of service.

On September 16th, 1925, the Atonement Seminary of the Holy Ghost was dedicated by Father Paul before a large group of clergy, university officials, and superiors of other religious houses. "I regard this as one of the most important forward steps the Society of the Atonement has taken in recent years," wrote Father Paul. And Mother Lurana rejoiced: "How very thankful I am that God has permitted us to live to see this great step forward for our Institute—a seminary for our Friars at the Catholic University." The foundress agreed to send her sisters to look after the domestic affairs of the seminary. As in the past, the two founders once more collaborated in bringing about a major development in the history of the society.

In the "roaring twenties" Graymoor itself was growing rapidly. When construction on the Little Flower Memorial Hall at Graymoor was begun in 1926, the cornerstone was laid in the presence of their Eminences, John Cardinal Bonzano, the Papal Legate to the Eucharistic Congress in Chicago, and Patrick Cardinal Hayes, the Archbishop of New York. Escorting the two cardinals around the Mount of the Atonement, Father Paul brought them to the Corpus Christi Cross which he had carried up the mountain through the wilderness many years before. Turning to Cardinal Bonzano, as they looked down into the lovely valley below, the founder asked: "Does it not remind Your Eminence of Assisi?" To be sure it did but on a smaller scale. Surveying the Mount of the Atonement they saw not only the original friary and the St. Francis Chapel but also St. John's minor seminary; St. Joseph's novitiate; St. Christopher's Inn; and the rising Little Flower Hall, which would provide offices, additional quarters for the friars, and a large auditorium for the use of the students. Probably that day Father Paul remembered more humble beginnings in an old paint shack. But he drew his faith from the covenant of old: "Surely blessing I will bless thee, and multiplying I will multiply thee." Graymoor was on the move.

During the early years that the society was part of the Roman Church, there was considerable progress made in stabilizing the community. Seeing that his more or less continual presence was needed, Father Paul made the decision never to accept a preaching assignment that would take him away from Graymoor for more than one night. Since he was an extraordinarily effective preacher in great demand, and since he saw this activity as an integral part of the ecumenical task for which he had founded the society, Father Paul was required to summon all his considerable resources of will and discipline in order to remain faithful to that decision over the years to come. Always restless, always zealous, he yearned to speak of the reconciliation, the At-One-Ment of men, but now he realized preaching had to be balanced with "pastoring" at home.

In fact, the emphasis of Father Paul's efforts from now on would be primarily centered upon internal affairs of the community and the Roman Church. This meant that he would no longer concentrate on things strictly ecumenical.

Instead, he frequently spoke from the sidelines about ecumenical events as his attention and energies were devoted more and more to governing his community and seeing that it took a respectable and accepted position within the Roman context of religious institutes. The choice was costly but necessary in view of the prevailing atmosphere in those early days of Graymoor's debut in the Roman Church. Still, he was not cut off completely from what was happening in the ecumenical movement within the non-Roman churches.

In 1914, for example, he reported to readers of *The Lamp* on the attempt of the Episcopal Faith and Order Commission to organize the World Conference that had been proposed by Bishop Charles Brent in 1910. Father Paul was especially pleased that a delegation from the conference was going to visit Pope Pius X. In an editorial he decried what was "a widely existing sentiment in Catholic editorial circles," namely a pessimistic view that "the proposed mission to Rome will result in nothing more than a desire to accomplish what, in existing circumstances, cannot be realized." True, said Father Paul, "any hope of immediate destruction of sectarian lines would be absurd." Yet, he continued, "who can it be that is urging on these prayerful and well-disposed men to bring about this conference and to labor for the ultimate reunion of Christendom unless it be the Holy Spirit Himself in energetic concert with Our Lord's own prayer, 'that they all may be one'." If the movement to form a World Conference and the decision to visit the Pope are the work of the Spirit, Father Paul asked, how could anyone despair of a favorable and fruitful outcome? Hence, he commended "this important Anglican delegation to the Holy See to the prayers of all our readers."

When the Protestant Episcopal Board of Missions decided to send seven delegates to the 1915 Pan-Protestant Conference in Panama which was making plans to dispatch Protestant and Anglican missionaries to the countries of South America, several members of the board resigned in protest of the decision. Among them was the Reverend William Manning, chairman of the Faith and Order Commission working to bring about the World Conference. Subsequently Manning was defeated for the office of deputy to the General Convention of the Episcopal Church. This was the first time that the rector of Trinity Church in New York City was defeated in an election for any office. Commenting on these events, Father Paul wrote:

As Chairman of the Commission that is laboring to bring about a World Conference on Faith and Order, Dr. Manning has demonstrated to the authorities of the Catholic Church by his recent action that he is sincere in the hope he has expressed that the conference in question might subserve the ends of Catholic Unity as distinguished from Protestant Federation, whose aim seems to be the coalition of all Protestant denominations in a united hostility to the Holy Catholic Apostolic and Roman Church.

In December 1920 Father Paul responded to Bishop Brent's report on the preliminary meeting of the World Conference on Faith and Order whose sessions were held at Geneva during August of that year. While agreeing with Brent's opinion that the movement for unity was "in the hands of God from whom it came and to whom it belongs," Father Paul found it necessary to explain to readers of *The Lamp* why the Pope declined an invitation to be represented at the conference:

It would be impossible for the representatives of the Pope to subscribe to the sentiments contained in this compromise of the whole question of Ecclesiastical Jurisdiction. If Our Lord Jesus Christ had to give to everybody without discrimination as to faith and order, a commission to "go Teach All Nations" and make disciples wherever, whenever, and in what way soever they could; if the bishops of the Orthodox, the Anglican, and the Methodist Churches, Presbyterian Elders, Baptist Ministers, and Y.M.C.A. secretaries were equally delegated by the Divine Master to convert the peoples of the earth, and no Supreme Shepherd was given such a thing as Universal Jurisdiction over all Christ's sheep, then Dr. Brent's condemnation of one church trying to attract to itself members from another church is not one bit too severe, even when he compares it to sheep stealing in the cattle world, which, he says, is held to be a crime. But as a matter of fact the Divine Shepherd, in order to preserve the essential Unity of His Flock, did the very thing which the Geneva Conference ignored, and which sooner or later future World Conferences must recognize, if ecclesiastical sheep stealing is to be abolished, and the entire body of Christ's sheep constitute but One Fold under one Sovereign Shepherd. . . .

If, therefore, the representatives of Peter's Successor had attended the preliminary meeting of the World Conference in Geneva . . . they would either have had to compromise the position of the Apostolic See by consenting to divide the conquest of the world for Christ to the various Missionary Agencies represented at the Conference, or else to withdraw in repudiation of the sentiment expressed therein on the subject of so-called sheep stealing. We say all of this not in wholesale condemnation of the Conference, but only to point out how entirely preliminary in its character the Geneva Conference actually was. . . .

This was, of course, 1920, and Father Paul reflected the thinking and mood of the Roman Church at the time. While he often wrote and preached about events similar to the movement of Faith and Order, he was no longer at ecumenical center stage after his reception into the Roman Church as he had been before it.

VII

How to be a Missionary and Never Leave Home

IN THE EARLY DAYS OF GRAYMOOR, Father Paul's brother, Charles Wattson, asked the question: "Where the hell is the institution?" Now there was an institution on the top of the Mount of the Atonement, and it had survived the catastrophic defections engineered by the society's first priest to be ordained after Father Paul. Over the years new recruits came to take the place of those who had left the little St. John's Seminary, and by the early 1920s Father Paul had a handful of priests to assist him. But the tiny institution which survived was a far cry from what its founder intended. He believed he had been called by God to found a great missionary order, yet he himself could not leave the

Mount to preach the Gospel for long periods of time because bitter experience had taught him that his firm hand of direction was needed at home.

Charlie Wattson's question had been answered about the institution, but now another arose: Where were the missionaries? Even an optimist like Father Paul had to admit that it would be years before his tiny community would be in any position to send out significant numbers of missionaries. All he could hope for was the chance to plant the vineyard which would later bear its harvest. In a nutshell, his problem was how to be a missionary and never leave home.

He had been turning the question over in his mind for a long time. Obviously he wanted his own friars to be missionaries, but were they the only ones who could carry the Gospel to the world? Could he support other missionaries in the meanwhile? Could lay people be involved in the spread of the Gospel? Was the mission of the Church the exclusive domain of its ministers?

In his Anglican days Father Paul had pondered the implications of what we would now call "Christian stewardship." On the feast of St. Thomas, December 21st, 1904, he awoke in his little cell at five in the morning as usual. In his mind he seemed to hear that same voice that had spoken to him before. "Gather up the fragments that remain, that nothing be lost," were the words that rang in his soul. They had been spoken originally by Christ to his disciples in the wilderness after a multitude of five thousand had been fed by him when he multiplied the five barley loaves and the two fishes. In obedience to the command of Christ, twelve baskets of food were gathered up by his disciples.

The thought that came to Father Paul, as he was put-

ting on his habit, was: "If the Christians of America could be trained to save for the Foreign Missions, the fragments which they carelessly throw away, or the many millions they waste and squander in ways that do not profit, an army of missionaries, sufficient to conquer the heathen world, could be supplied with all the material assistance needed for their campaign of missionary conquest." And again the whispering voice said to him: "You will have to wait seven years for this to be accomplished."

So began the foundation of the great "ammunition base" that Father Paul later established as The Union That Nothing Be Lost. He planned it as a missionary society that would supply all the material necessities for the front-line trenches, where the soldiers of Christ fight against the evils of the world for the salvation of the souls of men. Shortly after the inspiration came to him, he drew up the Rule and Constitution of The Union That Nothing Be Lost. He then made a diligent and persevering effort to enlist members in the Union among Anglicans, but his effort was a futile one.

Seven years later, in December of 1911, two years after the Society of the Atonement entered the Catholic Church, the Rule and Constitution of the Union was submitted to the Auxiliary Bishop of New York, Bishop Cusack, for his blessing and sanction. The Bishop said that he hesitated to bless it because the rule was so perfect he feared that the friars would find no one to live by it, and consequently it would be of no material gain to them in their good work. That answer came as a keen disappointment to Father Paul. At Mass the next morning, as he held the eucharistic Christ in his consecrated fingers before receiving Holy Communion, Father Paul prayed in these words: "Dear Lord—if

The Union That Nothing Be Lost is a creature of my own imagination, I beg you to dismiss it utterly from my mind; but if it comes as an inspiration from You, My God, please give me some tangible proof of it."

A few days later that prayer was answered in the person of a shabby looking old man who came to St. Paul's Friary asking to see Father Paul. When Father Paul entered the small waiting room, seeing the visitor, he thought that this man was another of the many poor, homeless men who came to the friary for food and shelter. Introducing himself as John Reid from Waterbury, Connecticut, he then told Father Paul the story of his life. It would never be considered interesting enough to be printed in the daily newspapers, but Father Paul saw in this man the answer to his prayer of a few days ago, and the very embodiment of The Union That Nothing Be Lost. John Reid's parents had left him a plot of rocky land in Waterbury; and for years he had worked hard to make it productive. The produce of this small farm he sold, spending the minimum of the money he realized from it on himself in order that he might give the maximum to God. In coming to Graymoor to see Father Paul—whom, he said, he considered a Christlike priest—he had ridden on street cars part of the way and walked the rest. For food he had with him a few sandwiches.

John Reid, in that conversation, asked Father Paul how he could establish a burse for the education of poor boys for the priesthood. Father Paul then told him of his desire, so long unfulfilled, of erecting in connection with the friary, a small seminary where poor boys could be educated for the priesthood. To Father Paul's amazement, John Reid offered to send 5,000 dollars, when he returned to Waterbury, toward the erection of the college. It seemed almost unbelievable that this shabby man, so lean and emaciated looking, should have 5,000 dollars. Did he really possess the money or was he just a visionary? Father Paul insisted that he remain at the friary overnight before starting his journey home.

Nothing more happened until a few days before Christmas when a letter dated December 21st arrived from Waterbury. Upon opening it, Father Paul found to his amazement that it contained a bank draft from Reid for 5,200 dollars. Pondering the odd figure on the draft, Paul saw here a symbol of the five loaves and two fishes with which Jesus fed the vast multitudes by working a great miracle. Looking at the letter again and noticing the date, he also realized that it was exactly seven years to the day, back in 1904, when he first conceived the idea of the Union That Nothing Be Lost.

No longer uncertain, Father Paul conducted a vigorous campaign in *The Lamp* to obtain new members for the Union. This time his efforts bore fruit, and he had many thousands of members by 1918 when the Union was incorporated under the laws of the State of New York. As a nonprofit organization, the Union was described thus in the papers of incorporation: "A missionary and charitable organization cooperating with the Society of the Atonement and having for its two-fold object corporal works of mercy and the salvation of souls. In furtherance of these ends it enjoins upon its members becoming self-denial and a holy simplicity of living, in conformity with their state of life, that nothing be lost which might be employed in extending the Kingdom of God or in ministering to the sick and poor."

As time went on and the Union grew, another organization, the Rock of Peter Foundation, also came into existence. Based on the annuity plan, the Rock of Peter Foundation employs the return from its investments solely in the erection of churches, schools, and orphanages both at home and abroad. *The Lamp* of February, 1927, outlined the purpose of the Rock of Peter Foundation as follows:

The Rock of Peter Foundation . . . is a one-million-dollar fund which the Board of Directors of the Union That Nothing Be Lost are trying to create for the benefit of the Universal Church, the interest of which is to be used for the extension of the Kingdom of God in all parts of the Catholic world; or else a certain portion of the fund is to be loaned *without interest*, to missionary Bishops and Religious Superiors for the erection of seminaries, churches, schools and hospitals, for a limited period of time.

Until his death, Father Paul distributed many millions of dollars through the Union and the Foundation to Roman Catholic missionaries, bishops, and religious orders all over the world. From 1911 to 1940 more than 3,000,000 dollars were disbursed through the Union alone. Even during the depression of the 1930s at least 100,000 dollars a year were given away at a time when the community itself was in severe financial straits. No request was ever declined by Father Paul as too large or too unreasonable. To him the Union and Rock of Peter Foundation were evangelical expressions of the ecumenical task to which his community was committed.

By aiding the needy of every creed or none, and not merely Roman Catholics, Father Paul felt that he and the society were fulfilling Christ's command to teach all nations so that the world might believe that He had been sent by the Father. Because Paul knew that it would be many years before it would become possible to send his own friars to the home and overseas missions, he was compelled by his personal zeal and his own interpretation of the ecumenical task to do something concrete in the meantime. He realized that a lack of unified action on the part of those who called themselves Christians was retarding the work of the Church, and he decided to organize a missionary union, "which seeks to gather together and absorb into itself fragmentary unity of humanity to abhor and sacrifice themselves for the worldwide extension of the Kingdom of Christ until all the nations of the earth are gathered into it and no soul for whom Christ died be lost." Why should this not be possible for Christians? he asked. After all, "this is a day of union of all sorts and kinds. We have great trust companies and financial corporations that are fast absorbing the wealth of the nation and in the field of industry the labor union. . . ."

Inspired by the conservation movement of his day, Paul thus stressed spending the minimum on self so that the maximum of time, talent, substance, and opportunity might be expended for others. Moreover, Paul gave special stress to the role of the layman in the missionary work of the Church. Time and again, he cited to the members of the Union the great good that was accomplished through the foundations established by laymen like John D. Rockefeller and Andrew Carnegie. It is not an exaggeration to say that Father Paul saw himself as a kind of ecclesiastical Rockefeller.

Just as the World Missionary Conference of 1910 in Edinburgh, Scotland, gave birth to the modern ecumenical movement, so also, in reverse, were the Union and the Foundation intimately connected with Father Paul's ecumenical vision of Church unity. For him *both* the movement for the unity of Christians *and* the propagation of the Christian faith were genuine expressions of his society's apostolate of bringing about the day when all men would be one. While work for Christian unity should not be confused with missionary activities, he felt that the two movements were intimately related as twin thrusts in the crusade to effect one fold under one shepherd.

Furthermore, over the years the Union That Nothing Be Lost provided the seed money for a number of projects which, as we shall see, grew to have worldwide influence within and outside the Roman Catholic Church. As a fund-raiser, Father Paul had few equals in the Roman Church. Though he never touched money, he surely could collect it. Money, like everything else, he believed, should be used to spread the Kingdom of Christ. Employing techniques like tithe clubs, self-denial weeks, running clocks, and miles of dimes, he prodded Christians to open their pocketbooks and donate to causes they had never heard of in places they had never seen. This, in itself, served a needed educational function by revealing to people the worldwide dimensions of being both human and Christian, particularly during an era of political isolationism and social insularity.

Although Father Paul accomplished much for the domestic and overseas missions, he was not alone in his efforts. On the home front various organizations like the German Catholic Central Verein and the American Federation of Catholic Societies attempted to raise the social consciousness of American Roman Catholics. In 1910 Father

William Kerby and a number of others founded the National Conference of Catholic Charities to bring order to Roman charitable endeavors. After World War I, the National Catholic Welfare Conference organized a Social Action Department under the direction of John A. Ryan, the "Right Reverend New Dealer." And on a different level, Dorothy Day and Peter Maurin began their Catholic Worker Movement in the early 1930s. Overseas, the chief representative of American Roman Catholic mission efforts was the Catholic Foreign Mission Society of America, more popularly known as "Maryknoll."

What Father Paul contributed was a popular technique for engaging the interest of the largely indifferent mass of American Roman Catholics in causes which transcended their own Church and nation. The activities of the great national organizations, and even the personal witness of people like Dorothy Day, had very little immediate effect among the majority of American Roman Catholics. But Father Paul had the unusual ability to speak to the "grass roots" and to evoke a generous response from ordinary folk who knew little about Christian social theory and witness but who recognized in others needs like their own—hunger, disease, poor housing, and a host of other ills. It was Paul's charism to be the catalyst for their empathy and charity.

Of all the needs to which Father Paul responded, his favorites were probably those concerning the medical missions. Certainly such requests absorbed more pages of *The Lamp* than any other cause, and in describing them Father Paul rose to the height of his notable eloquence. Around the early part of 1913, Father Paul preached the Three Hour Service on Good Friday at St. Denis's Church, Yonkers, New York. During his talk on Jesus' brief cry "I thirst," he had made a strong plea for support of the overseas missions. When the service was over, he met a certain Dr. Paluel I. Flagg, a young physician from Yonkers, who expressed a desire to become an overseas missionary. After speaking with the founder, who confirmed him in his intention, Flagg, a few days later, corresponded with Father Paul and proposed the establishment of a Catholic Medical Missionary Propaganda which would send trained physicians as well as priests and sisters to China, India, and Japan. Agreeing that this plan would meet a severe need, Father Paul placed the pages of *The Lamp* at Flagg's disposal to see if something more concrete would result.

In May 1914, the first announcement of the formation of the Propaganda was made, and in June of the same year Dr. Flagg wrote to the founder: "I know that you will be glad to hear that your article on the 'Catholic Medical Missionary Propaganda' has already borne fruit." What had happened was that Dr. Margaret Lamont of Ashcroft, British Columbia, had contacted Dr. Flagg and offered to set out for the mission fields if the money for passage and maintenance could be found. At almost the same time another woman physician, Dr. Mary Rouchel of Croghan, New York, wrote to say that she would provide financial assistance to send a woman doctor to India. Flagg put the two women in touch with one another. The result was that Dr. Lamont, a former Anglican, became the first Roman Catholic woman physican to work in the overseas missions under the sponsorship of the Catholic Medical Missionary Propaganda. As her field of endeavor she chose China where she had labored for many years while an Anglican.

Shortly thereafter, Dr. Flagg changed the name of the Catholic Medical Missionary Propaganda to the Catholic

Medical Mission Society which in turn became the medical branch of the Union That Nothing Be Lost. Eventually the Medical Mission Society was named the Catholic Medical Mission Board under the direction of the Father Edward Garesché, S.J., who continued to make appeals through *The Lamp*. Thus, for the first time in the American Roman Catholic Church there existed an organization which concentrated its full resources on supplying medical supplies and personnel to the overseas missions.

This development was another indication that American Roman Catholics, both clergy and laity, were becoming conscious of human misery in other lands and beginning to realize their responsibility to meet those needs. Because of internal problems in the Church, such as the horrendous task of absorbing the great masses of immigrants who arrived in the late 19th century, American Roman Catholics had spent most of their time and energy up to the early 20th century on national and internal needs and had thereby narrowed their religious horizons. Indeed, only in 1908 had Rome developed enough confidence in the ability of the American Church to hold its own that the Vatican officially removed the designation of the country as "mission territory." The Catholic Medical Mission Board was, then, a sign that American Roman Catholics were maturing and taking up their duties as Christians for others outside their own ghetto. They were beginning to have an ecumenical vision, however limited it still was.

In 1934 Father Garesché sponsored the establishment of a religious community of sisters called Daughters of Mary, Health of the Sick, whose foundress was a former Sister of the Atonement, Sister Angela, S.A. Sister had worked for a number of years along with other Sisters of

the Atonement at the first headquarters of the Catholic Medical Mission Board in a loft on Broadway in New York City. There she caught Father Garesché's enthusiasm for the medical missions and, since the Sisters of the Atonement did not do that kind of work, decided to leave and form her own community. Unfortunately, because of the lack of vocations and overwhelming financial instability, the community of sisters ceased to exist after about 25 years, although their male counterparts, the Sons of Mary Missionary Society, also sponsored by Father Garesché, are today promoting the work of medical missions in the United States and abroad. From that chance meeting of Father Paul and Doctor Flagg, three significant institutions devoted to the sick and the dying around the world were established.

At a meeting of the Catholic Medical Mission Board held in 1926 at Manhattanville College, New York, Father Paul, a member of the board, was introduced to one Anna Dengel. A physician, Miss Dengel was interested in forming a religious community whose apostolate would be solely the medical missions. When the new Society of Catholic Medical Missionaries was being established a few years later by Mother Dengel, she asked Father Paul to use an empty building behind the Atonement Seminary in Washington, D.C., for the first motherhouse of her community. Although he declined her request since he needed the building himself, Paul did give Mother Dengel 25 dollars each month for a period of several years to be applied toward the rental of another house. And when a new motherhouse for the medical missionaries was being built, Father Paul appealed in *The Lamp* for 500,000 bricks to erect the building. On hearing of Father Paul's death,

Mother Dengel wrote: "Our little Society owes a deep debt of gratitude to your venerable founder, because from the very beginning he was in sympathy with our work and gave it moral and also financial support." A decade after his death, Mother Dengel further reminisced that "when we started our Society, very few people sensed the meaning of medical missions. Father Paul did. I count it as a great privilege to have known Reverend Father Paul, and I hope he is continuing to keep an eye on the medical mission movement in which he was so very interested."

Medical missions, however, were not the only object of Father Paul's generosity. Month after month, hundreds of missionary appeals consumed pages of fine print in *The Lamp*, and there was always one short article headlining a particular appeal with titles like "Resolved: That We Build a New Church for Father Collins in Sour Lake, Texas"; "Will Father Arnold Witlox, C.M. of British East Africa, Ask in Vain?"; "An Appeal for a Chapel"; "Poor Clares (of Rome) Close to Starvation"; "Father Rossi, S.J., Needs a Motor Boat in the Yukon"; "Uganda Missionary Needs Five Hundred Dollars to Build a School."

Father Paul's efforts to enlist Christians in the work of unity and missions was not limited to adults. There was a Union That Nothing Be Lost chapter of the Holy Childhood Association, and in *The Lamp* a special column devoted to children was edited by "Aunt Helen." Of its many activities, the chief apostolate of the association was "the ransoming of pagan children," and Father Paul was an ardent supporter of the work. Replying to an irate reader who insisted that it was impossible to "offer a pagan soul for the release of your own soul," Father Paul explained in *The Lamp* what was meant:

In pagan lands life is not considered as sacred and precious as in civilized countries. For various reasons thousands of infants are cast off every day to die a lingering death; often babies are put to death. Many of these are ransomed by the Missionaries for a small sum of money. In sections where the killing of babies is a more or less common practice, the Missionaries engage trustworthy natives to gather in the little castaways; also the Sisters try to gain access to sick children and frequently baptize those that are dying. To enable Missionaries to carry on this work and care for the infants snatched from an untimely death or left on their hands, people are wont to make an offering of Five Dollars. It entitles them to be godparents for the little infant and select the name it shall receive in Baptism. Pagan baby benefactors are credited with making these unfortunates children of God through Baptism. If they die, they have a faithful intercessor in heaven; if they live, they share in all the good that is accomplished. Not only zealous Missionaries and Sisters go forth from these Holy Childhood Orphanages, but the countryside is dotted with Christian villages round about the Mission compound, where the one-time castaways are the happy fathers and mothers of numerous Christian households.

You ask an explanation of the sentence, "Offer a pagan soul for the release of your own soul." It is this. We owe a certain debt to Divine Justice for the sins we have committed. We may not enter heaven until that is paid. The ransom of a pagan soul is a great act of charity which may release the soul of the pagan baby benefactor from Purgatorial pains. Scripture tells us that "Charity covereth a multitude of sins." If you ransom a child who dies immediately after Baptism, that child in the enjoyment of the Beatific Vision will not forget the great gift of the benefactor who made such enjoyment of Our Divine Lord possible. Its prayers will certainly ascend to Our Lord during your life upon earth and after your decease, that you may likewise, purified from all taint, enjoy the destiny of the Saints.

So things went with the Union until Father Paul was able to announce in 1928 that "The Union has scored its first million of contributions for the extension of the Kingdom of God at home and abroad; and is reaching out for greater achievements in support of the missionary work, not only of the Friars of the Atonement but of other Catholic missionaries . . . , whether it be in Asia or in Africa or in the Islands of the Sea." A million dollars raised in less than 17 years. This was a magnificent accomplishment, particularly since it happened before the days of highly sophisticated Madison Avenue techniques in advertising, the rise of direct-mail professionalism and the advent of computer technology. Paul's achievement was, however, fully in accord with his strong belief in the philosophy of rugged individualism and laissez-faire economics, though in this case on behalf of religion.

One of the islands of the sea where the founder helped to build a new church was in the Philippines. At Baguio the magnificent Church of Our Lady of the Atonement was slowly being erected, and in 1922 Father Paul ran a campaign to collect over 100,000 dollars so that the church could be completed. Though the campaign, like many others which he conducted, was not completely successful, nevertheless over 4,000 dollars were sent to the Very Reverend A. Van Zuyt, the provincial of the Belgian Mission Fathers who ran the parish at Baguio. This is just one example of hundreds of buildings Father Paul helped to erect all over the world.

Some appeals for funds conducted by Father Paul exceeded their goals, however. One of these was not for an overseas mission or even a domestic mission but rather for a need right in Father Paul's backyard. In Peekskill, New York, about five miles from Graymoor, the single Roman Catholic parish there, the Church of the Assumption of

Our Lady, was laboring under an enormous debt for so small a village with its many citizens of very limited financial capabilities.

In the center of the village of Peekskill stood what was called the Guardian Building, a Gargantuan pile of rather undistinguished architecture. It was, as Father Paul reminded the parishioners, "a monster parish building outclassing anything of its kind even in New York, the biggest city in the world." Built in the early part of the century to serve as a parish school, hall, and social center, "The Guardian," as the locals called it, had been constructed during the tenure of the Reverend Dr. James T. Curran and in the regime of Archbishop John Farley of New York. So large was the debt that the parish could barely meet the interest payments, much less reduce the principal of the loan.

When Dr. Curran died, the burden of these heavy financial responsibilties fell on the shoulders of a frail, holy priest, Reverend Richard Tobin, the next pastor. By then, things were really in financial disarray. Summing up the situation, Father Paul described the poor state of affairs thus: "Nobody but one who stood in the same place could exactly understand the terrible mental strain, the anguish of soul, the constant appeal to God for help which must have been experienced by Father Tobin during those long weary years when it fell to his lot to meet the interest payments on 'The Guardian' which were continually coming due. Besides the mortgage debt he had to face an endless succession of notes, which with the inexorable exactness of the almanac kept summoning him to the bank on a certain date. And no sooner was one payment made than the next interest date immediately stared him in the face, and this went on month by month and year after year and with the revolutions of the calendar the burden of debt never grew one whit less."

In desperation Father Tobin finally appeared at Father Paul's doorstep to ask his help in finding a solution. Together they decided to use *The Lamp* to appeal for funds. The initial request fell flat. What happened next was this, according to Father Paul: "Then we hit on the project of *Building* a *Mile of Dimes*. It was Father Tobin's idea, not mine. I simply adopted it as the best method of appealing to our people, and you know how the readers of *The Lamp* all over America responded to that appeal. Prior to Father Tobin's death, over one hundred thousand dimes had been contributed. Not long ago the first reduction on the principal of 'The Guardian' debt was made by a draft on the Mile of Dimes."

Shortly before his untimely death, Father Tobin received a very attractive offer from a theatrical company to buy "The Guardian" and convert it into a school for actors. Clearly the parish was not yet out of the financial woods, and Father Tobin was strongly tempted to accept the offer. In order to have the building, Father Tobin, with the aid of Father Paul, submitted to the Archbishop of New York the following proposition: "A united effort to be made in five years' time to wipe out the entire remaining debt of four hundred thousand dollars; the whole archdiocese to assume the responsibility of raising a million and a half of dimes in that period of time, provided the congregation would raise a million and a half, and *The Lamp* one million dimes in addition to the one hundred thousand its readers had already contributed."

For some reason the archbishop was cool to the idea

and declined to participate. Nonetheless, the prelate "was sympathetic to such a degree that *The Lamp* volunteered to do its share in any case." So appeals for the Guardian Building continued in the pages of *The Lamp* for many years after Father Tobin's early demise. To add some incentive to the readers, Father Paul promised that if the full 100,000 dollars was raised by the feast of the Assumption of Mary in August 1921, he would send any surplus to the Poor Clare nuns in Rome to help build a new monastery for them. Not only was the goal met by August 15th, 1921, but also the Poor Clares were recipients of a 5,000 dollar gift from the readers of *The Lamp*.

Father Paul's munificence, made possible through the alms given by the readers of *The Lamp*, was, of course, not confined to needs at home or in the Far East. At the end of the First World War, thousands of Greek, Armenian, and Russian refugees fled the Crimea in the wake of reported Bolshevik persecution. Many of them went to Constantinople, which, naturally, was unable to absorb such great numbers readily and provide them with proper food and shelter. Conditions soon became unspeakable. Informed of the situation, Pope Pius XI ordered Bishop George Calavassy of Constantinople to proceed to the United States on a fundraising tour so that sufficient money might be raised to relieve the plight of the people of the Near East.

A prelate of the Eastern rite in union with Rome, Calavassy was also a close friend of Father Paul who had been providing the bishop with alms for some time through the Union That Nothing Be Lost. Calavassy had met Father Paul in 1918 when, as a monsignor, he had toured the United States to raise funds for the suffering people on the island of Siris in the Mediterranean. Because of the terrible conditions in Constantinople, however, the bishop was unable personally to fulfill the Pope's mandate. Instead he chose as his substitute an Irish priest, a much decorated chaplain of the British army, Monsignor R. Barry-Doyle, who at the time was stationed in Constantinople. Unfortunately Barry-Doyle knew hardly anyone in America, and he asked the bishop for names of people he might contact there before beginning his lecture tour. Bishop Calavassy knew one name very well—Father Paul's.

On November 25th, 1922, therefore, the monsignor arrived at Graymoor where Father Paul mapped out a fund-raising campaign for him. In the December issue of *The Lamp*, Paul made the blunt announcement that because Barry-Doyle's mission had been ordered by the Pope, he was calling upon the readers to contribute to Near East relief the sum of at least one million dollars, an extraordinarily large amount in those days. Almost as an aside, he mentioned that the project could be completed very quickly and the monsignor could soon go home again if every reader would contribute only two dollars each. Indeed, he suggested, if every subscriber would instead send ten dollars each, then the monsignor could go away with two million to lay at the Pope's feet. It was all as simple as that for Father Paul.

1923 sped by while Monsignor Barry-Doyle lectured throughout the United States and Canada and spoke in places like the Grand Ballroom of the Plaza Hotel and Carnegie Hall, New York City. In the first issue of *The Lamp* for 1924, Father Paul was able to announce that "the gross receipts from the Monsignor's lectures, and contributions to his fund through the medium of *The Lamp* and the Union That Nothing Be Lost during 1923, have totaled more than forty thousand dollars." There was a long way to go before reaching even the first million dollars but that did not discourage Father Paul. He knew what great good could come from the donation of even a few dollars to any cause.

From his correspondence with Bishop Calavassy in the year previous, he was aware of what had been accomplished by spending much less than 40,000 dollars because the bishop had written: "More than half of the expenses for the maintenance of our missions, schools, nuns, seminary and clergy was afforded by *The Lamp* and The Union That Nothing Be Lost, which proves how beneficent is your work to the Church and to the cause of reunion. . . . Thanks to your assistance we have been able to increase the number of our Sisters, of our seminarians and of our clergy, . . . to build a new chapel, to enlarge our school buildings, to bring the number of our students to 540 and to receive into the church 335 converts." Such progress must not be halted, Father Paul felt, merely because of a lack of funds.

To insure a continuous and organized program on behalf of the Near East among American Roman Catholics, Monsignor Barry-Doyle and Father Paul decided, therefore, to incorporate the work under the title of The Catholic Near East Welfare Association with headquarters in New York City. Barry-Doyle became the first president of the corporation while Father Paul was named vice-president as well as a member of the board of directors whose chairman was Bishop M. J. Hoban of Scranton, Pennsylvania. In the fall of 1925, Barry-Doyle went to Rome with a full report on the affairs of the association. This he presented to the Pope, and after his audience he also conferred with a variety of high Vatican officials. To all, of course, he mentioned Father Paul's work for the association through the medium of *The Lamp*. Reporting on his visit, Barry-Doyle wrote to Father Paul: "Very few American Catholic periodicals are as well known in Rome as *The Lamp*."

In the United States and collecting funds for the needy at nearly the same time as Monsignor Barry-Doyle was a Benedictine priest from Austria, Father Augustine Count Von Galen. Brother to Clement Von Galen who would become Bishop of Muenster, Germany, and a formidable opponent of the Hitler regime, Father Augustine was touring the United States to obtain money to aid the Russian refugees in the city of Vienna, Austria. With the permission of his superiors and the special approval of the Pope, Von Galen formed a society called the *Catholica Unio*, or The Catholic Union, whose purpose was not only to help the refugees, but, further, to educate priests of the Eastern rites who would work to reunite the refugees with the Roman Church eventually.

Father Paul also sponsored the work of Von Galen, for we find Mother Lurana writing in her diary: "Reverend Father had a meeting with Dr. Von Galen whom he is assisting to launch his great plan to save the faith in Russia by erecting seminaries in Austria for the education of Russian young men to return to their home-land as priests. Father is advocating the union of the Institute with the Near East Welfare Association. Both of these organizations have Papal approval and to both our Father has been a 'Providence.'" Indeed Mother was correct. Father Paul was working very hard to form one unit of two groups which had somewhat similar goals.

When the founder went to Rome in 1925, one of the purposes of his visit was to secure papal approval of a plan to merge The Catholic Union and The Catholic Near East Welfare Association. This merger was proposed in order to avoid confusion among the faithful and also to make possible a concerted effort that could utilize all the personnel and, more important, all the funds collected by the two organizations. In 1926, through an official papal letter, the work was greatly expanded and placed under the direction of the Holy See and the bishops of the United States. Pius XI directed that, "in view of the personal interest hitherto manifested in The Catholic Near East Welfare Association by His Eminence Patrick Cardinal Hayes, it seemed well that he should be designated as Protector of the enlarged association, for which title 'The Catholic Near East Welfare Association' will be sufficient to express adequately the general purpose and scope of these two unified organizations." Thus, the papal letter continued, "the title includes also The Catholic Union and the purpose for which that Society has hitherto labored."

In effect, the work of Augustine Von Galen had been swallowed up by its more powerful counterpart, and his organization was given a name that hardly typified its chief concerns. Vienna, and even Russia, is a long way geographically and psychologically from Constantinople. Nevertheless, at a September 29th, 1926, meeting of the new association, the group went through the motions of electing as president the Reverend Edmund A. Walsh, S.J., rector of the School of Foreign Service and vice-president of Georgetown University. Walsh had been the personal representative of Pope Pius XI in a relief mission to the Russian people. In view of the delicate nature of relations between the Vatican and Russia at the time, as well as because of Walsh's genuine professional expertise, this appointment by the Pope was obviously a reward for Walsh's services to the Vatican. Once Monsignor Barry-Doyle was out of the picture, it is perhaps surprising that Father Paul was again elected vice-president of the association.

In 1927 the American bishops at their annual meeting passed the following resolution:

The Hierarchy of the United States in conference assembled to express their full approval and adoption of the program of the Holy See providing for the unification of all societies now working in the United States of America for Russia and the Near East. The resultant organization, The Catholic Near East Welfare Association, Inc., shall be the sole instrumentality authorized to solicit funds for Catholic interests in those regions and shall be so recommended to the entire Catholic population of the United States simultaneously in all dioceses on a given Sunday, the date to be arranged in consultation with the respective Ordinaries.

Commenting on the action of the bishops, Father Paul wrote in *The Lamp*:

Under the blessing of God enormous results ought to follow . . . now that the Holy Father has created The Catholic Near East Welfare Association into a Pontifical Society and at the will of the Supreme Shepherd all the Cardinals, Bishops and Priests of America will henceforth both sanction and support it. As for the Catholic faithful of our country there is no question of their following where their shepherds lead the way . . . for the proper carrying on of this enormous work that has to do with the return of one hundred and fifty million stray sheep of Orthodoxy to One Fold under One Shepherd.

This comment of Father Paul reveals how much he reflected his times. Papal approval, once given, would definitely insure the success of any project, considering the extreme ultramontanism of the American clergy and laity at the time. Roman Catholic laypersons were often regarded as sheep who should follow their ecclesiastical shepherds wherever they led. The shepherds, it was felt, had superior knowledge on almost every matter. Ecumenism consisted of any work that achieved, or held the promise of achieving, the return of all the lost sheep who, it was insisted, had to belong to the One Flock, the Roman Church, under the One Shepherd, the Pope, at the peril of their souls. However outdated many of these concepts may seem today, it should be evident that Father Paul espoused most of the reigning ideas in the Roman Church of his era.

As for Father Paul's part in founding The Catholic Near East Welfare Association, which still exists today and promotes throughout financial and moral support greater understanding among Christians of the Near East as well as reconciliation between Christians and non-Christians, Mother Lurana perhaps described it as well as anyone when she wrote:

Father has been tireless on behalf of the great work of Bishop Calavassy's Near East Relief—not only for rescue but for reunion—for it is such in its appeal and effect upon the Orthodox Church in Constantinople. As both Bishop Calavassy and Monsignor Barry-Doyle have declared many times, our Father was and is the great factor in its success here, and co-founder of the Catholic Near East Association. It was to Father that the Bishop sent Monsignor when he came to this country friendless. Father introduced him and encouraged him and gave largely to him. He did his utmost to disarm hostility and indifference and went in person to assist him. I have myself heard Monsignor Barry-Doyle state in a sermon that without Graymoor and Father he would have been helpless. I wish to place this on record now, when, thank God, many others are helping and the end—success—is in sight.

It is ironic that in spite of, or perhaps because of, the accomplishments of Father Paul in the overseas and domestic missionary arenas, he was able before his death to send his friars to only a few places that could possibly be considered "missionary" situations. One of these was St. Anthony's parish in Hereford, Texas. The Sisters of the Atonement preceded the friars there. In fact, it was in Hereford that the sisters made their first foundation outside of Graymoor. Several factors urged Mother Lurana to send her spiritual daughters to this spot which, in 1917, was extremely isolated. First, the Roman Catholic population of the area was tiny and had been the object of a good deal of anti-Roman propaganda. Second, the people were extremely poor and unable to meet the expenses entailed in maintaining a parochial school with a well-paid staff. The poverty, if anything, would have attracted the Mother Foundress in any case.

Shortly thereafter, the friars took over the administration of St. Anthony's parish in Hereford and today continue their labors after some 50 years among the Mexican-Americans and Anglo-Americans of the region. In 1938, when control of the parochial school was able to be assumed by other religious, the sisters left Hereford. Before his death Father Paul also saw his friars begin work in Vancouver, British Columbia, among the Japanese there, and in Kinston, North Carolina, among black people. This was the entire extent of the outreach of the friars' mission-

ary apostolate until 1940, but it was at least a partial fulfillment of Paul's words in an early issue of *The Lamp*: "By
the law of consequence and dedication it follows that a
Society called into being to promote the mission and work
of the at-one-ment must be, *ipso facto*, a *missionary*
Society."

Though he was constantly concerned for the growth
of his own community's missionary work, Father Paul was
nonetheless very generous in referring young men and
women to other religious communities as well. For example, a former black Episcopal clergyman whom Father Paul
had received into the Roman Church was having trouble
during 1928 in finding a Roman seminary that would admit
him for priestly studies. In a letter to the provincial of the
Society of the Divine Word, Father Paul remarked with
reference to the former clergyman: ". . . it is a source of
deep distress to me that a man of such talent and ability
who desires to serve God in the priesthood of the Catholic
Church should meet with so many obstacles which exist
only because he is a negro and not a white man. Had his
color been white and he had come from the Episcopal
Church with the same record and education to his credit,
there would have been no difficulty whatever of his being
received either by a religious community or by the
Bishops for the secular priesthood. We all recognize that
fact. After all, is the Episcopal Church less prejudiced
against the colored race than the Catholic Church which
claims to be the Church of all races that they can ordain
and provide a rectorship for a man of Mr. Fitzpatrick's education and ability whereas the Catholic Church has no place
where he can serve his own race as an evangelist and a
priest?" For the late 1920s this was still a rather daring ques-

tion to ask in the Roman Church, but Father Paul's strong sense of the universality of Christian mission helped him to transcend the ingrained prejudices of American Roman Catholics in his day.

Thus, in so many ways the missionary par excellence, Father Paul never really left home. But he helped countless thousands to find their rightful place in the family of man and in the household of those who believe in Jesus and his meaning for the world. That *all* may be one was no idle dream for Father Paul.

VIII

Lighting Lamps and Candles in a Darkened World

AS WE HAVE SEEN, PAUL'S FIRST JOURNALISTIC INITIATIVE was the founding of *The Lamp* in 1903. While *The Lamp* has a rather fascinating history after the reception of the society into the Roman Church in 1909, perhaps even more can be learned about Father Paul the journalist from his involvement with another quite different magazine. The periodical concerned, unlike *The Lamp*, was not a creation of Paul's. Its original objectives were not those of *The Lamp*, and its reading audience was unfamiliar to Paul. How the founder assumed control of *The Antidote*, changed its goals and at the same time had his own horizons broadened, constitutes a significant note in the history of Roman Catholic journalism in the United States.

Down in the panhandle of Texas, about 50 miles southwest of Amarillo, an elderly Roman Catholic priest, Reverend J. A. Campbell, was doing his best to serve the scattered parishioners of his vast parish which stretched 100 miles in each direction from the main center at Hereford. Once a Presbyterian, Father Campbell was devoting his talents to the Roman Church despite his advanced age and a bad heart condition. Moreover, Campbell was trying to counteract the intense and vicious anti-Roman propaganda that was being spread by newspapers like *The Menace* and *The Yellow Jacket*. These papers were distributed free to every mailbox throughout the countryside of northern Texas on a regular basis and were gradually poisoning the minds of the farmers and ranchers around Hereford. Campbell knew he must do something before the situation grew worse.

About 1910 Campbell purchased the old Deaf Smith County courthouse. He used one of the rooms in the building for a chapel and a second to house a printing press. The press served a twofold purpose. Since the parish was small and unable to pay the debt on the old courthouse, the income from printing could be applied to the mortgage. And *The Antidote*, which Campbell published there, was intended to "nullify the poison distilled into the minds and hearts of the people of the southwest by the unspeakable *Menace*." Using a hand press and working as long as 18 hours a day, Campbell managed to publish *The Antidote* by himself for nearly seven years. Eventually, however, the task became too much for the old man and he was forced to seek aid.

From reading *The Lamp* and from personal acquaintance with the founders, Campbell knew about the work for

Christian unity being done by the friars and sisters. So in early 1917 he asked Mother Lurana to send her sisters to conduct the small parish school and help at the printing press. Responding to his appeal, Father Paul first sent two tertiary brothers of the community to assist with the printing. Then Mother Lurana dispatched four sisters on August 27th, 1917, to run the school and care for the office work at the press. Less than a year later, Father Campbell was forced to retire temporarily from active duty because of his poor health. Fortunately he made arrangements with Father Paul to continue publication of *The Antidote*.

In October 1918, Father Paul began printing *The Antidote* in New York City in order to relieve the overburdened sisters in Texas. Later he moved the entire operation to the Guardian Press in Peekskill, New York. The changes in the masthead during the early years reveal how the purposes of *The Antidote* changed after Father Paul gained control. In 1918 the magazine was published "in the interests of Catholic Church Extension in the South and Southwest, U.S.A." After June 1919 it was issued "in the interests of Church Unity and Christian Democracy." In the middle of 1923 those words disappeared, and instead the goal of *The Antidote* became "to establish a line of communication across the gulf of separation that lies between the Holy Roman Catholic and Apostolic Church on one side and the Protestant, Anglican and Orthodox denominations on the other." Further, its aim was "to discuss in the spirit of friendliness and reconciliation the differences that now divide us and thereby to prepare for the final establishment of the Kingdom of Christ in the whole world, including God's Ancient People who are destined to be numbered among the worshippers of Jesus Christ. . . . " Regular features in *The Antidote* were "Echoes of the Press," brief news notes of ecumenical interest; "The Antidote Forum," a question and answer column written by Father Paul; a "Jewish Page"; and "The Home Circle," the latter was accompanied by a picture of a typical American Roman Catholic family of seven seated in their Victorian living room in front of a fireplace graced by a large painting of the Sacred Heart of Jesus.

In the April 1924 issue of *The Antidote* there was an announcement on the inside front cover entitled "Graymoor Village in the Making." The advertisement described Graymoor Village as a "colony of Catholics who, with modest incomes can, nevertheless, erect bungalow homes which, at a moderate cost, can yet be made beautiful and artistic so that the whole may constitute a residential park like the suburban villages of which there are so many . . . in New Jersey and on Long Island." Graymoor Village was an example of what Father Paul understood as "Christian Democracy." Based primarily on the social encyclicals of Pope Leo XIII, the concept of "Christian Democracy" was as much economic as it was political in character. And for Father Paul, the existence of a small village of cottages owned by clean-living, solid citizens of "modest income" and grouped around a monastery in truly medieval fashion was a microcosm of what the world could and should be. Although Graymoor Village never amounted to much, the project is indicative of how Paul conceived the relationship between Christianity and the socio-political realm.

"Christian Democracy" was, moreover, the answer to the threat of communism, according to Father Paul. In an article entitled "St. Francis of Assisi and Christian Democracy" Paul explained to readers of *The Antidote* how the

Poverello had helped to "break the backbone of the feudal system of the Old World." By forbidding the members of his Third Order to swear the oath of military service to their overlords, St. Francis deprived the feudal masters of power to make war, argued Father Paul. Thus, he continued, were laid "the foundations of the liberty of the people which eventuated in the rise of popular Government in Italy, France, England and ultimately in the great free States of America." In the 20th century, Father Paul maintained, the faith and spirit of St. Francis were needed more than ever because the world must be made safe for democracy:

But what kind of democracy is to exercise its sway over the Old World as well as the new? Is it to be a Bolshevist democracy or a Christian one? The struggle of the future . . . is between Jesus Christ and the devil for the mastery of the Democracy of the world and it is going to be a bitter struggle. . . . Bolshevism, rising like a nightmare in the East, is the reign of Hell on earth, under the Red Flag of Socialism. . . . The Red Book of Socialism, recently discovered in New York, reveals a system of organization which has behind it the intelligence of Hell, and unless the Christians of all denominations can get together and stand shoulder to shoulder, resisting the onward march of Socialism with its doctrine of infidelity, destruction of capital, and overthrow of government, we are in great danger of being worsted in the fray.

One additional reason for the unity of Christians, wrote Father Paul, was to halt the spread of the "Red Menace" and ultimately defeat it.

Just as there was a "Lamp Army," so there were "Antidote Crusaders." The crusaders were described as "an association made up of the Catholic subscribers of *The*

Antidote who, by their loyal and united support of the magazine will make it more effective in realizing the noble objects for which it is published, opposing the hatred and bigotry inspired by Anti-Christ against the Church with the spirit of Christ Crucified that seeks by 'telling the truth in love' to help the Good Shepherd fulfill his ancient prophecy: 'Other sheep I have which are not of this Fold under One Shepherd.'" The crusaders were automatically members of the Union That Nothing Be Lost, and to them Father Paul often addressed appeals for missionary needs as well as the many building projects of the society.

Occasionally Father Paul placed items of special interest to friends of Graymoor in *The Antidote*. One of these features was a history of the Society of the Atonement. Another was the second revised edition of *Prince of the Apostles*, which Paul had originally coauthored in 1908 with the Reverend Spencer Jones when both were still Anglicans. In *The Antidote*, Father Paul wrote his history of the society under the nom de plume "E. U. Lex." In *The Lamp*, he edited the memoirs of Mother Lurana, also under the same pseudonym. Apparently, an exaggerated sense of religious modesty as well as a desire to be stylish in the best tradition of British writers caused Paul to take up this rather strange custom. Here it should be noted that much of the material in *The Antidote* was not written by Father Paul but by Mr. J. A. M. Richey, a former Anglican clergyman and associate editor of *The Antidote*. Because Paul seldom signed editorials or even entire articles, one can often say only that certain ideas are in the spirit of his thought and not directly attributable to him.

Besides Bolshevism, one of Father Paul's special targets was the Ku Klux Klan. Nearly every issue of *The Anti-*

dote contained articles, news reports, and editorials denouncing the Klan. An editorial entitled "Christmas and the Ku Klux Klan: An Address to the Protestant Clergy" is typical. Here is how the Klan is described:

Not content with a promiscuous press propaganda, Lucifer has organized an invisible empire of men who operate in the dark and behind masks for the avowed purpose of guaranteeing that the United States of America will always be dominated and run politically, socially and morally by Protestant white men; that Negroes, Jews and Catholics are to be cowed into subservience to this same Protestant white majority by the decrees of secret Klaverns and hooded juries, whose sentences are to set at naught the judgments of the Civil Courts, whenever there is any clash between them, and the executioners of the mandates passed by the invisible "Sanhedrin" shall be night riders who can handle the whip, the rope and the tar brush with a savage brutality that will strike terror into every man, woman and child. . . .

In appealing to Protestant clergy who received *The Antidote* at a special cut-rate subscription price, Father Paul related his denunciation of the Klan to the movement for Christian unity. "No obstacle," he continued, "has risen up in the way of Christian fellowship and Church unity in the whole history of the United States so serious and diabolical as the Ku Klux Klan; and in harmony with the angels' song at Bethlehem . . . we call upon our brethren of the Protestant clergy to oppose the further progress of Colonel Simmon's Invisible Empire."

Like *The Lamp*, *The Antidote* did not confine itself only to the fight against anti-Roman Catholicism or to the crusade for the unity of the Christian Churches. Political events, both international and national, received frequent attention. During the 1920s and 1930s one of Father Paul's deep concerns was the anticlerical government in Mexico and the reported persecution of the Roman Catholic Church there. Linking the Calles administration to Anti-Christ and godless Bolshevism, Father Paul reserved some of his strongest language for the denunciation of Calles whom he called a "merciless anti-Christian Tyrant, now outclassing Nero, Diocletian and Julian the Apostate in his fiendish assaults upon the Catholic Church." In reaction to the situation south of the border, Paul appealed for funds to transport a number of priests and sisters from Mexico to the United States. Moreover, he called on his readers to pray fervently: "Do not such unspeakable atrocities stir your heart and soul to their very depths and ought not the knowledge of such barbarities . . . urge us to pray and ask of God to show us what we can do in befriending our persecuted fellow Catholics and bringing this intolerable tyranny to an end?" In order to educate and inform non-Roman Catholics concerning the Mexican problem, Father Paul urged his Roman Catholic readers to subscribe to *The Antidote* for at least one other person not of the Roman faith.

Furthermore, Paul urged the readers of *The Antidote* to send newspaper editors the following letter: "Dear Mr. Editor: Why is it that you print all the news from everywhere except from Mexico? Why is it you have no editorial word to utter against the inhuman barbarities perpetrated in that country against its best citizens for religious and political reasons. . . . Thousands of your readers don't understand your silence. Please tell us the reason why." Father Paul's interest in the Mexican cause remained strong throughout the life of the magazine.

On the home front Paul frequently directed the attention of his readers to national political developments which he felt had some relation to the crusade for Christian unity and Christian Democracy. Commenting on the defeat of Alfred E. Smith for President in 1928, for example, Paul wrote:

It was undoubtedly Protestant opposition to a Catholic becoming President of the United States which was the most powerful factor in Mr. Smith's defeat. If the Democratic Party cannot rise above the religious intolerance and hatred which has displayed itself in this campaign it will never again be great enough to command a majority vote of the American people. Consequently its national power and influence will degenerate into political impotence. The decline of the Democratic Party will inevitably be followed by the rise of a new power in the nation—Sovietism. As the Goths and Vandals made their inroads from the North, laying waste the civilization of Ancient Rome, anti-Christian Socialism now threatens America. The Christian forces of the nation, hopelessly divided into hostile camps, Protestant and Catholic, will hardly be able to cope with this dreadful scourge and enemy of our Christian Civilization. . . . May unchristian malice die the death it rightly deserves and brotherly love in America everywhere prevail.

Once again Paul interpreted a national event in the context of Christian unity. One also suspects that he voted Democratic in 1928, something he did not do very often.

Besides political matters, *The Antidote* was filled with comment on what Father Paul considered the leading moral abuses of the day. When two Episcopal rectors in the neighborhood of Cold Spring, New York, a small town near Graymoor, reportedly addressed a meeting of the American Birth Control League, Paul attacked the rectors for having "loaned the weight of their ministerial position in the community to a propaganda that is in conflict with the Divine Law of both nature and revelation." Continuing his charge, Paul lamented:

King Herod has been execrated by twenty centuries of Christian thought as the murderer of Innocent Babes. Alas that those who profess to be ministers of Christ and preachers of His Holy Gospel should, however unwittingly, join the successors of Herod who in every age and generation since the birth of Christ have carried on the slaughter of the Innocents. For they who murder *unborn* infants or encourage others by preaching the false gospel of Birth Control to carry on the traffic of prenatal infanticide are to a greater or less degree *participes criminis* with bloody Herod. . . .

In the very next column was an article entitled "Appalling Results of Birth Control," and at the bottom in small print were the words: "Atheists in the pulpit do not represent the heart of our country."

Anyone who incurred Father Paul's wrath was subject to denunciation. Objecting to a piece in the *New York Times* authored by Mary Burt Messer, a professor at the University of California, Paul deplored the fact that Messer advocated the substitution of "idealism" for religion as the key to saving family life in America. Paul answered:

When those, who are given to rationalism in theology and naturalism in philosophy, declared their doctrines of emancipation, those who acclaimed their teachings never considered for one moment the consequences of such seed being sown in the popular mind. At present we realize all too well to what extent the family and the home have succumbed to the noxious influence of those doctrines. But we are still far from admitting that for the family, too, there can be no other than the one laid by the Divine Savior. . . . Filled with the same pride which possessed the philosophers of Athens who considered it fatuous to give ear to St. Paul, she (Miss Messer) proclaims: "Science and sociology must come to the aid of the foundering American family." God save the mark! If the American family can find no better savior than these, its doom is sealed. Science and sociology may aid those who are anxious to reform the family to perceive more clearly the problem in all of its ramifications. But they really cannot solve the question since it is not given to them to instill new life into a corrupting body. The chief hope of the American family, as of any family, is the Divine Savior in whom all things may be and must be reformed and reconstructed.

Noting that there were an estimated one million drug addicts in the United States during the early 1920s, Father Paul asserted that recent research showed that "not more than half of our physicians realize that drug addiction is a disease" and that "the theory that it is 'a vice' is still largely taught in schools of medicine." As a result, drug addicts "became so innocently—many by having opium in some form prescribed by their own medical men." Addressing the readership, Paul gave the following advice: ". . . we earnestly recommend the readers of *The Antidote* to keep a sharp lookout in case of sickness or the undergoing of an operation not to be doped by hypodermic injections beyond a very few times and only then when the limit of human endurance without morphine to induce sleep has been reached. . . . This section of *The Antidote* is devoted to the Home Circle," he continued, "and one of the simplest and surest ways to introduce hell on earth into the Home Circle is for their father or mother, son or daughter to become a Drug Addict. Beware of opiates!'"

Another danger to family and country was what

Father Paul called "John Barleycorn." He always had a horror of alcoholic abuse and its effects. Spiritualizing this fear, he made abstinence from alcohol one of his chief suggestions for self-denial to members of the Union That Nothing Be Lost. Moreover, he made certain that abstinence from alcohol and tobacco, the latter of which he called "the Weed," became regulations in the constitutions and rule of the Society of the Atonement. Such prohibitions were removed from the use of tobacco in Father Paul's lifetime (much to his sorrow), and from the use of alcohol after his death. While they were in effect, the regulations were often violated by the friars. Contradictions of his ideals caused him to react excessively at times, so great was his zeal for self-denial in the cause of Christian unity.

There is the story, for example, of a friar, just a few months from ordination to presbyterate, whom the rector of Atonement seminary caught smoking tobacco. The deacon, now one of the senior priests of the society, was about to be dismissed from the seminary by Father Paul when the rector intervened and imposed a stiff penance that suited the founder. The deacon's penance was to eat supper kneeling on the floor of the dining room for a month.

Moreover, Paul was convinced that the mere existence of a law did not guarantee that the desired effect would be achieved. The Volstead Act, which prohibited the sale and use of alcoholic beverages, is a case in point. As far as Father Paul could see, the Volstead Act was not being adequately enforced since "the saloon still exists, and, judging from local observation, in a more pernicious form than it did before." In the village of Peekskill, New York, Father Paul cited three saloons still in operation. The only real change was a higher price for drinks. It was foolish, Paul maintained in *The Antidote*, for reformers "to think that all that is necessary to eliminate an evil is to pass a law to prohibit the thing we deplore." What then was the answer? Why, it was for the reformers to "busy themselves in seeing that the law is enforced, at least to the degree of protecting the laboring man from the outrageous robbery to which he is subjected by the publicans who still perpetuate the saloon and make it even more the gateway to hell than it was before." Again, the money spent on alcohol, tobacco, and other luxuries could be put to much better use, Father Paul felt.

When Paul heard that some women were buying hats for as much as 40 dollars apiece, he declared in *The Lamp*: "Such a hat must be a very heavy burden on a woman's head and conscience, if she knows that with that forty dollars she could have saved eight or nine Chinese babies from being devoured by dogs. . . ." Writing to members of the Rosary League another time, he exclaimed that "beauty parlors are transforming our decent Catholic women to look like modern Jezebels." What was needed, he said, was "a crusade for reform in dress, reform in manners, reform in pursuits, and a change from the worship of the creature to the Creator."

Paul constantly inveighed against excess in the use of creature comforts, some of which admittedly were legitimate. But it was for a greater good, namely, the extension of the Kingdom of God on earth and the unity of the Christian Churches, that the serious disciple of Jesus abstained from goods of a lesser nature—less for self and more for God. This type of asceticism was familiar to many American Protestants but for Roman Catholics it must have seemed unthinkable, undesirable, and unworkable. Father Paul nonetheless persisted in propagating his ideas in *The Lamp* and *The Antidote*.

In 1919 Father Paul purchased his own printing press at the Guardian Building in Peekskill, New York. There he printed *The Lamp*, *The Antidote* in both a northern and a Texan edition, and any outside orders that he could obtain. Finding that production of two editions of *The Antidote* was most inconvenient and a needless expense, the founder decided to dissolve the Antidote Publishing Company in late 1921 and combine the two editions of *The Antidote* into one national magazine beginning in 1922. In February 1931, because of severe economic conditions, *The Antidote* was merged with *The Lamp*, and some of the more popular features, like "The Antidote Forum," were incorporated into the older publication. By the time of the merger, Father Paul had obtained several hundred thousand subscribers to *The Lamp* and had established a thriving publishing business.

At the same time he announced the purchase of an old music conservatory on Ringgold Street in Peekskill, a building which he converted into a new home for The Atonement Press. His explanation of the name for the press is an illustration of how he conceived his place in the world of Roman Catholic journalism:

It (the property) was recently purchased as the permanent home of The Atonement Press, which name we have given to our printing plant, not only because it is to be the publishing headquarters of the Society of the Atonement, but because the title tells to the world what the special mission of this printing plant is, namely, *Atonement*, or *Reconciliation*, first of all between God and man, through those who have been redeemed by the Blood of Christ with each other. For, it is the purpose of The Atonement Press to promote unity and good will among the Children of God and to help destroy those enmities of 400 years standing between Catholics and Protestants at which angels weep and devils laugh. Whereas Satan is working his printing presses day and night to perpetuate the hatreds engendered by the Reformation between Christian Brethren, and to stir up Protestants against their fellow citizens by the propagation of venomous slanders and lies; we only desire to make effective in the 20th century the words which Saint Paul addressed in the 1st century to the Ephesians: "But now in Christ Jesus, you, who sometime were far off are made nigh by the Blood of Christ. For He is our peace, who hath made both one. . . ."

From The Atonement Press, which later became known as The Graymoor Press, Father Paul also issued the annual called *The Graymoorian* which had been inaugurated in 1921 by Mr. J. A. M. Richey, associate editor of *The Lamp*, to give Richey's seminary students at Graymoor some practical experience in editorial writing. Beginning in October 1923, the friars started publishing a companion and booster for *The Lamp*, which was called *The Candle*. Because the economic situation was so bad in that year, subscriptions to *The Lamp* declined drastically. So Father Paul began *The Candle*, which was smaller and less expensive, and promoted it with the slogan: "If you have no *Lamp*, take a *Candle*." Eventually the Sisters of the Atonement took over *The Candle* and used it as an organ for promoting the Rosary League and fostering vocations to their community. *The Candle* ceased publication in the 1960s due to the sisters' heavy financial commitments elsewhere.

After the merger of *The Antidote* and *The Lamp* in

1931, Father Paul concentrated his journalistic efforts chiefly on publishing *The Lamp*. Although his original intent for the magazine was to promote Anglican-Roman Catholic reunion, as time went on the scope of *The Lamp* widened to include Christians of every denomination. This was in keeping with the words of Christ "that *all* may be one" which were printed on the bottom of every page of *The Lamp*, at first in Latin and later in English. In *The Lamp*, Paul continued to encourage prayer for unity, especially during the Church Unity Octave, later known as the Chair of Unity Octave, and called on Christians for support of the worldwide mission of the Church through the Union That Nothing Be Lost. After Paul's death in 1940, *The Lamp* became a Roman Catholic family magazine, thus reflecting the low state of interest in ecumenism among American Roman Catholics during the 1940s and 50s.

In the 1960s, at the hightide of ecumenical interest, *The Lamp* recaptured its original purpose as a grass-roots magazine promoting the unity of all Christians. Sadly, the magazine was forced to cease publication in the early 1970s due to overwhelming financial problems. Over the years *The Lamp* published articles by such ecumenical notables as Father Bernard Leeming, S.J., Augustine Cardinal Bea, Archbishop William Baum, Bishop John Mormon, Dr. Martin E. Marty, Archbishop Michael Ramsey, Father Herbert Ryan, S.J., Dr. J. Robert Nelson, and John Cardinal Willebrands. With such a broad spectrum of authors and ideas, *The Lamp* was a faithful mirror of the ecumenical movement's growth and development during the 20th century.

Because Father Paul keenly perceived the importance of employing every possible form of communication to propagate At-One-Ment among men and to encourage the unity of the Christian Churches, he was not content to use his pen only. In 1935 when one of the friars, Father Anselm De Pasca, proposed a weekly novena to Mary on the radio, Paul willingly agreed to the project. After consultation with broadcasting officials in New York, Father Anselm decided that instead of novena devotions it would be better to dramatize the lives of Christian saints. Nonetheless, the program would still be called the *Ave Maria Hour* even though the Marian theme would receive minimum attention in the programming.

On April 28th, 1935, the first broadcast, narrating the life of St. Mary of Egypt, made its debut. This novel project of educating listeners in the values, message and lives of Christian heroes and heroines had immediate success, and the number of radio stations subscribing to the service increased dramatically. Only a few years after its inception, the *Ave Maria Hour* was being broadcast over more than 100 stations with millions of listeners. During its 35 years of broadcasting, the program inspired and consoled men and women of many faiths or none, all the while trumpeting the message of reconciliation of men with men, and of men with God. For Father Paul, electronic journalism was one more human creation that could be employed to break down the barriers erected by ignorance, prejudice, and hatred. By lighting *The Lamp* and *The Candle* and beaming the *Ave Maria Hour* throughout America, Father Paul made a darkened world torn by war, depression, and injustice a better and more hopeful place in which men could work out their reconciliation. To one of his radio audiences Paul once said: "I have always been taught by several practical experiences that prayer is not only efficacious, but necessary. God wills and expects us to pray, and if we will not ask, then we need not expect Him to give." Having received abundantly himself and being grateful for it, Paul indeed prayed without ceasing.

Nowhere in the life of Father Paul is his conviction that the Spirit was guiding him more apparent than when he discussed his task of preaching the Word of the Lord. In a letter to an inquirer who had asked him where he had attained his knowledge of prayer, Paul replied:

If you have been listening to my sermons over WMCA for any length of time, you must have noticed how full they are of quotations from the Old and New Testament. My mind is so saturated with the word of God that they come to the surface spontaneously in my preaching. In fact outside of the radio I don't think that I have written out three or four sermons for delivery in the course of my lifetime. I always preach extemporaneously and do so in conscientious obedience to the instructions our Lord gave His Apostles when He sent them out, saying: "Take no thought what ye shall say for in that hour it shall be given you what to speak, for it is not you that speaketh but the Spirit of your Father that speaketh in you." I have been especially devoted to the Holy Spirit all my lifetime, and He has led me marvelously more and more into the fullness of divine Truth.

Not only was Father Paul an outstanding preacher but he was also a man of intense prayer. Despite all the demands on his time, he was faithful to the regular routine of prayers followed by the other members of the community, and he spent long hours at night before the Blessed Sacrament. A reminiscence by one of the senior friars of the community perhaps illustrates the true attitude of Father Paul toward his work and prayer. The friar writes:

Because the cell which I occupied for about three years was

directly opposite that of Father Founder, I became familiar
with how he spent much of his time. Occasionally he would
rise about 2 A.M. and go to work in his office which was on the
ground floor of the old friary. His excuse for this was, "Well,
we must get *The Lamp* out." So he would write without
interruption until meditation time at 5:30 A.M. Ordinarily he
went to bed on time. Twice I went into the chapel after 10:30
P.M. and found him on his knees before the tabernacle, and said
to him, "Father, it's time to go to bed." His only answer was,
"All right," and immediately he went to his room—like a tired
child might do.

Of course, Father Paul continued to encourage other
Christians to pray also, particularly for the unity that is
willed by God for the Church. As has been noted, his
efforts centered mainly on promotion of the Church Unity
Octave, which he began in 1908. Upon Father Paul's
reception into the Roman Church, Pope Pius X gave his
blessing to the octave. In 1916 Pope Benedict XV extended
its observance to the universal Church through an apostolic
brief. The octave was thus no longer a private devotion
but prayer that was approved for the entire Roman
Church. Benedict's papal brief gave great impetus to the
observance of the octave throughout the world, so much so
that Father Paul was encouraged to enlist the support of
bishops everywhere to make the octave obligatory throughout the Church, "in the same manner as are the prescribed
devotions to the Blessed Virgin during the months of May
and October."

When Father Paul went to Rome in 1925 he carried
with him petitions signed by 200 bishops and over 5,000
priests, religious, and laity asking that the Octave be univer-
sally obligatory. By 1928, he was able to report that "there
are now about nine hundred and fifty prelates who have

signed the petition, including three of our four American cardinals." Support for the desired goal grew, and on the Feast of St. Anthony, June 13th, 1929, the petition signed by over 1,200 prelates was presented by Father Paul's representatives at Rome to Cardinal Laurenti, the Pro-Prefect of the Sacred Congregation of Rites. Though cordially receiving the representatives, the cardinal said: "You ask a difficult thing." There was strong doubt in the cardinal's mind that the Pope would accede to Father Paul's request.

In June, 1930, the Sacred Congregation of Rites informed Father Paul that his petition was denied until there was further proof that the Octave was so widely observed and supported throughout the Church that it could be prescribed for all. Needless to say, this would require a new, intensive campaign for support. He was just not up to such a mammoth undertaking. Replying to a priest in Rome who urged renewed efforts, Mother Lurana explained why this was not possible.

First, Father [Paul] has not the men to delegate for such an extensive and prolonged affair. . . . As Father grows older every moment of his time is taken up with increasing responsibilities and active duties of his growing congregation. . . . And as the Institute is still young we have not anyone . . . who can be told to go ahead and manage the affair, nor do I think it would be completed in an average lifetime.

Nonetheless, Paul continued to spread the observance of the Octave by correspondence with bishops and through *The Lamp* until his death.

A few years before the adverse decision of the Sacred Congregation of Rites regarding obligatory observance of the octave, Father Paul gave the prayer movement a subtitle

—Chair of Unity Octave. The subtitle emphasized the papal character of the unity for which prayer was offered, the "chair" referring to the Throne of Peter, from which papal authority over the Church was exercised. Moreover, the new title distinguished the octave from all other prayer efforts for unity among Protestants. Still, Father Paul did see that most other Christians could not participate in the octave as long as it was specifically oriented toward the "submission" of non-Roman Christians to the Holy See. In a letter written the year before his death, he suggested that Orthodox, Anglicans, and Protestants could pray "in a general way that unity be brought about."

Such an expansion of the concept behind the octave was realized in 1935 through the efforts of a Roman priest of the Archdiocese of Lyons, France. Like Father Paul, Abbé Paul Couturier had an ardent desire to promote the unity of Christians. Unlike him, Abbé Couturier urged Christians to pray that God would bring His children into perfect unity at the time He wills and by the means He wills. The more general scope of Couturier's movement, without the heavy papal emphasis, thus made it possible for Christians other than Roman Catholics to participate in prayer for unity without violating their consciences.

Beginning with the 1920 Conference on Faith and Order in Geneva, Protestants, Orthodox, and Anglicans had, of course, been promoting their own week of prayer for unity each year. In 1941, Faith and Order changed the dates of its observance to coincide with the Roman observance during January. In the years after the deaths of Father Paul and Abbé Couturier, a certain rivalry among Roman Catholics grew up between those who favored Father Paul's pro-Roman observance and those who espoused the movement inspired by Abbé Couturier. Frequently the division went according to geographical lines. In France, Germany, and the Low Countries the format inspired by Couturier was extremely popular, while the papally oriented octave had more adherents in English-speaking and Latin countries.

The difficulty for Roman Catholics ceased with the promulgation of the Decree on Ecumenism by the Second Vatican Council in 1964 by which the condemnation of common prayer for unity was reversed. Roman Catholics could now pray with other Christians in certain special circumstances, such as prayer services for unity and in ecumenical gatherings. Thus in 1966, for the first time in many centuries, Christians of all denominations were able to join together in a common Week of Prayer for Christian Unity. That Christians pray *at all* for unity in January each year is due to the inspiration of Father Paul. That *all* Christians may now pray together for the unity which God wills in His own time and in His own way is the realization of Abbé Couturier's dream.

Father Paul always considered the corporate reception of the Society of the Atonement into the Roman Catholic Church as the "first fruits" of the Week of Prayer which he founded. Shortly thereafter, the Anglican Benedictine Monks of Caldey, Wales, founded in the late 19th century by Dom Aelred Carlyle, were also corporately received in 1912, as were an associated group of Benedictine nuns the following year. Dom Carlyle, a friend of Father Paul's, attributed his community's reception in "large measure" to the prayers offered during that unity week.

In the December 1909 issue of *The Lamp*, Father Paul expressed his heartfelt hopes for the Anglicans and invited them to turn to Graymoor for help and encouragement, especially in the matter of entering the Roman Church. "We are much too grateful for our own admission to the Fold of St. Peter not to stretch out a loving hand to every individual soul, who is contemplating the same step with a glad cry of help and encouragement. We want all our dear old Anglican friends and brethren to know, that wide-opened arms and a heart brimful of joyous welcome awaits everyone of them, who now or hereafter, turn towards Graymoor seeking us as a medium of entrance into Peter's ship."

Five years after the admission of the Society of the Atonement into the Roman Catholic Church, Father Paul wrote:

We do not expect a corporate submission of *all* Anglicans to the Apostolic See, in either this or any other subsequent generation, but we *do* anticipate the home-coming of the Catholic Remnant. How extensive the numbers will prove to be God alone knows!

Toward the end of his life Father Paul apparently began to realize that there was no immediate prospect of large corporate reunions with Rome. It is true that in 1930 the Syrian Jacobite bishop in India, Mar Ivanios, began a mass movement of that Church to Rome, so that in a space of a few years a majority of the original independent Church were given autonomous status within the Roman communion while retaining their own rite. Yet for the most part the Churches were as divided toward the end of Father Paul's apostolate as they had been when he began many years before.

Consequently, he changed his stand, which he had held

as an Anglican, against individual as opposed to corporate conversions, and began to advise those Anglicans who sought his advice to immediately make their own reconciliation with Rome rather than await that long-hoped-for day of the corporate reunion of the two Churches. In the year before he died he wrote: "I am positive if you submit yourself absolutely to the guidance of the Holy Ghost, asking Him to enlighten you concerning the Papacy, He will guide you into all truth and in doing that will bring you after the manner of the Founders of the Atonement Institute into the 'One Fold under the One Shepherd'." He went on to tell the inquirer that "you would render the Episcopal Church the best service possible by getting into the Catholic Church and uniting with us in our prayers and efforts. ..."

Perhaps the hope for corporate reunion, which as we have seen has been revived as a viable goal for Roman Catholics by the Second Vatican Council, seemed further away than ever to Father Paul at the close of his life. One hopes that he found consolation in his own words, written while still an Anglican: "Were the mountains of difficulty to be surmounted a thousand times higher and vaster than they are, God is able to cast them into the sea. Faith serenely rests her case with him."

IX
Life With Father Paul

THOSE WHO SPOKE OF FATHER PAUL both in the Roman
Catholic Church and outside of it, as "erratic," "eccentric,"
and "abnormal" were persons who had never met him. He
once attended a Catholic function, and seated at the very
same table was a priest who had attacked him in his parish
monthly. The priest's name happened to be mentioned at
the table, and Father Paul, not realizing that the priest was
sitting there, said to the priests at his table: "My, my, I
hope Father ——— soon turns me and *The Lamp* over on
his gridiron for we are quite scorched on one side." By the
charm of his personality and humor and the utter lack of
any bitterness on his part, Father Paul turned what might

Greeting Graymoor pilgrims

have been an unpleasant experience into a joke. It was not until after he left the table that Father Paul learned that the priest who had attacked his life's work had broken bread with him. When he returned to Graymoor he told the story of the incident, much to everyone's amusement. Those who had the pleasure of knowing Father Paul knew him for the perfectly normal, gentlemanly priest that he was. Those who had doubts about him seemingly never bothered to verify them.

Because he was so natural and so normal, however naïve at times, he was delightful to live with. To the day of his death he took part in every activity of the friars and students. The older friars knew that Father Paul had a cardiac condition and they were always on the alert, especially when he was no longer young, to spare him any extraordinary exertion. But, like all active and busy men, he would not spare himself. There is an amusing narrative of a friar coming up the Mountain in 1939 and seeing, to his amazement, Father Paul, who was then 76 years old, playing tennis in the hot sun in his habit with three young seminarians. It took some real diplomacy to stop the game, and to convince Father Paul that it was not because of his health or his age or his ability to win but because the sun was too hot for the students—which it was—not to speak of for himself.

The recreation hour was spent on summer evenings on the lawn playing croquet. Father Paul liked croquet but he disliked losing any game to his friars. If he lost he pouted. Apropos of croquet there is a humorous incident in Father Paul's life which is another manifestation of his complete naïveté. In the summer of 1933, when Father Paul was not feeling well, he spent a few days at Long Beach, New

York. His companion was another priest who had made an engagement with some friends to play golf at the Lido Club, but he had to leave for New York without being able to notify them. When they arrived, Father Paul opened the door. The friends of the priest explained about the appointment for the game of golf. Father Paul told them what had happened, and then he asked, "What is the game of golf like?" When they explained the intricacies of golf, he said, "Why, it's just like croquet; will it be all right with you if I go?" They said that, of course, it would be a pleasure. So off they drove to the fashionable Lido Club, with Father Paul wearing a red flannel shirt, a cap, khaki trousers, suspenders, and high top shoes.

When they reached the first tee and handed Father Paul a club to tee off he turned to them and said: "I forgot to tell you, I am a southpaw." So back to the clubhouse went one of the men, who happened to be a banker, for a bag of left-handed clubs. The caddie-master said that there was only one set there and it belonged to a member who probably would come out to play that day. "Give me the clubs," said the banker, "and tell him that Father Paul is using them." The caddie-master said, "This man doesn't know Father Paul; he's a Protestant." Finally the manager was sent for and it was explained to him that the famous Roman Catholic priest, Father Paul, founder of Graymoor, was waiting for a left-handed set of clubs to tee off on the golf course. The manager graciously took the responsibility of lending the clubs, and Father Paul finally teed off. In relating the story at Graymoor he said, "My golf companions were very courteous; they let me carry my ball over the water hazards." The story of Father Paul's first—and last—golf game has often been told in the Bankers' Club of New York. Aside from the hazardous episode of the left-handed golf clubs, Father Paul's golf companions have often said that it was one of the most delightful afternoons of their lives.

During the very difficult days of the economic depression which gripped the United States during the 1930s, Father Paul carried a heavy burden in trying to provide for a fast-growing community. A Jesuit priest spent some time at Graymoor as a guest of Father Paul during those trying days, and in an effort to divert Father Paul's mind from so many cares, the Jesuit prevailed upon him to learn how to play cards during the recreation hour. He learned the game called "Five Hundred." The older friars and the good Jesuit, knowing Father to be a "bad loser," always let him win. However, when he played with the novices on Wednesday evening, which he always did, he sometimes lost, which was something he did not like. Father Paul, as the supreme head of Graymoor who had borne the burden and heat of the day before most of his friars were born, just could not endure losing in chess or cards or croquet to his friars. It was a human failing, but one found in many great men.

Neither did Father Paul like to see the students in the minor seminary—St. John's—or the friars in the major seminary lose a baseball game to another seminary. For years there was a baseball game scheduled between St. John's minor seminary at Graymoor and the major seminary of the Foreign Mission Society of America—Maryknoll. The founders of both societies were intimate friends.

For years the score did not vary much. It was usually Maryknoll 12, Graymoor 2. However, in May 1934, through some oversight in arranging the schedule, Maryknoll found that they were booked to play another seminary on the same day that a game was arranged with Graymoor. Not to disappoint Graymoor, Maryknoll sent its second team for the game. The result was that for the first time in six years Father Paul's boys defeated Maryknoll.

Father Paul was so delighted that he gave the following account of the victory in the June, 1924, issue of *The Lamp*:

The Maryknoll team came to Graymoor for the annual baseball game on Wednesday, May 16. This game always stands out as the most important one of the season. For six years running the Maryknoll clerics have defeated the St. John's team. This year the tables were reversed. The battle on the diamond started at two o'clock and finished at half past four. It proved to be one of the most thrilling games we have ever witnessed, and the tension increased as the game drew to its conclusion.

At the start the St. John's boys had the lead with a score of four to one, but when Very Reverend Patrick Byrnes, Vice-President of Maryknoll, and Father Francis Winslow, Assistant General, arrived on the ball ground during the fifth inning, their presence gave the Maryknoll boys a new lease on life, and they fought desperately from that time until the end to overcome the lead of the Graymoorians. When the ninth inning came the score was three to four in favor of Graymoor.

Peter Katsuno, our Japanese pitcher, struck out two of the Maryknoll batters, and then the third one sent the ball sailing out into the right field and two men got their bases. Whether those men on bases would succeed in reaching the home plate, thus giving the lead to the Maryknollers, was of supreme interest. Our Peter rose to the emergency, however, and struck the third man out, thus giving the game to Graymoor.

Father Paul was 71 years old when he described the baseball game so vividly in *The Lamp*. He held that same enthusiasm for all the student activities until he died six years later.

An interesting and amusing sequel to the story of the baseball game was told by the Father General of Maryknoll, the Most Reverend Raymond A. Lane, 15 years later, when he came to Graymoor on the occasion of its Golden Jubilee. In telling of the friendship that had existed between the founders of Maryknoll and Graymoor, Bishop Lane recalled the story of the baseball game.

Bishop Lane was rector of the Maryknoll Seminary at the time the game was played. When Bishop Walsh, the founder of Maryknoll, read Father Paul's account of the game in *The Lamp*, he asked the rector for a report on Maryknoll's defeat. When the circumstances were explained to him Bishop Walsh said: "I do not mind the defeat as much as I mind Father Paul's publishing an account of it in *The Lamp*." Bishop Lane concluded the story by saying: "Wasn't it wonderful, that our two founders, despite their preoccupation with many important affairs, and despite, or maybe because of, their evident sanctity, always remained human enough to be keenly interested in the victories and defeats of the ball teams representing their schools?"

As Father Paul strove for perfection, it was apparent to all who were closely associated with him that the imperfection he struggled with most was a quick temper, or the disposition to become angry. Sometimes in his sermons, as he condemned the evils of the day, his anger would flare up just as it did in his office when he was annoyed by some friar's infraction of the rule. But the inward struggle in the soul of Father Paul against this imperfection was so great that at times it manifested itself outwardly in the quivering of his lips.

As he grew older, his friars, knowing that he would

not touch money, were careful in arranging for someone to accompany him wherever he went. But sometimes he would suddenly decide to go to New York from his office at the convent, and he would be gone before they knew it. To forestall his suffering humiliation, a commutation ticket on the New York Central Railroad from Peekskill to New York was kept in his coat pocket. This solved the train-fare problem but it did not solve the subway or bus-fare problem, which Father Paul begged from passersby as he needed it. Before he asked anyone for his fare he always said one "Our Father." Even when he was given the fare by some kind person, there was the problem of his not handling it. So he would have the person either drop the coin between the pages of his breviary or into an empty envelope. When the turnstiles were erected in the subways and on buses, another problem was to get the conductor or agent to drop the coin in the slot for him. Fortunately, Father Paul met up with many Roman Catholics, who saved him the pain of being rebuffed by those who would not understand.

On a trip to the major seminary in Washington, Father Paul and his friar companion stopped off at Philadelphia to see the sisters who had a mission among the blacks of that city. Resuming the journey, railroad tickets to Washington had to be bought and a telegram sent to the Washington Superior as to their arrival. At the telegraph office the clock showed that there was very little time before the train left. Father Paul's companion asked him if he would write out the telegram, and before leaving for the ticket office he deposited a dollar bill on the counter. Later when Father Paul met him at the train he handed him a neat little yellow package. It contained the change from the dollar bill, which Father Paul had the attendant wrap in a telegram blank.

Because of his compliance with the private vow he had made never to touch money, Father Paul, particularly in his Anglican days when he constantly wore his habit, suffered many humiliations. Once, when he was an Anglican clergyman, he accosted a man to pay his subway fare. The man, looking on Father Paul in his habit, said: "Why, you lazy monk; I wouldn't give you a red cent!" The "lazy monk" at that time was doing enough work to keep four men busy.

In the last ten years of his life Father Paul was spared this humiliation by the constant vigilance of the friars and the sisters. Only once did he slip away and at that time, for some reason or other, he did not have even the commutation ticket. The station agents of the New York Central Railroad, however, took care of the situation and were later reimbursed by the friars.

In a little book found after his death there is a record of self-accusation for having allowed a friar to persuade him to take a taxicab instead of a street car one hot day in Washington. They were visiting the major seminary at Catholic University. The little book told the story of how the fare was spent unnecessarily through a permission Father Paul gave to the friar.

The Poverello of Peekskill, as one writer called him when he died, ever strove to follow in the footsteps of the Poverello of Assisi. Cardinal Dougherty of Philadelphia, writing of Father Paul on October 16, 1945, stated:

. . . I was struck by his eloquence, the clarity of his discourse, and the ease with which he delivered it. One could not help being struck forcibly by his profound spirit of poverty in which he seemed to emulate the Poverello of Assisi; and this was not the only outstanding quality of St. Francis of Assisi that he strove to practice. He transferred from the thirteenth century to the twentieth century the religious fervor which characterized the Middle Ages.

In later years, being constantly occupied with many big problems, Father Paul became forgetful of little things. He was constantly losing his breviary whenever he left Graymoor. He came in on the New York Central one day shortly before he died, and was met by one of the friars at the station. "Well," Father Paul said with a smile, "I left my breviary on the train again." The friar assured him that it was quite all right and that he would seek it in the "Lost and Found Department." "I went in there," Father Paul said, "to report the loss of my breviary, and I left my brief-case on the counter; so you will have to retrieve both of them." Once he walked off a Third Avenue elevated train, leaving his breviary, and that one was never recovered.

As founder of the Society of the Atonement, Father Paul was the personification of the society's rule of life. Like most religious communities the friars rose at five A.M. No matter how quickly after rising the young friars could reach the chapel, Father Paul was always already there kneeling before the Blessed Sacrament, a gray-brown figure before a white marble altar illuminated by a flickering sanctuary lamp. The points for the half-hour meditation, which always began at five-thirty, were often given extempore by Father Paul on some phase of the Atonement of Christ, or on some special graces which God had showered upon the Society of the Atonement. Often he would present a very down-to-earth meditation such as the ones he often gave on the difficulties of monastic life. "If," he once said, "you think you will get used to rising at five o'clock in the morning and like it you are very much mistaken. I am over seventy and I have not gotten used to it yet. But the sacrifice you make pleases God and brings down His Mercy upon a sinful world; and console yourselves, for in Heaven there is no weariness. There we shall always be refreshed as we participate in the infinitely active life of the Blessed Trinity."

Father Paul loved the major feast days of the liturgical year. The great events in the life of Christ, the feast days of the Blessed Mother, and of the other patrons of the society were days of special rejoicing. After the solemnization of the Divine Mysteries, the joy which exuded from Father Paul's own personality pervaded Graymoor through the day. At the noon and evening meals there was always some extra item of food, and talking was permitted during the meal; never, however, at breakfast, since the great silence which always began at Graymoor after night prayers did not end until after breakfast. In the evening of a great feast day the students would put on a minstrel show or a debate, which Father Paul always attended with a deep interest. He liked the debates best since they helped to develop the talents of the future preaching friars.

Father Paul particularly loved the Feast of the Transfiguration, celebrated on August 6th. On that feast day in 1934, after intoning the Gloria of the Mass, he stood before the tabernacle seemingly lost in the joy of the occasion, and instead of sitting down at the president's bench he continued to sing in Latin with the choir, in his deep, resonant voice, the words of the Doxology, "We praise Thee, we bless Thee, we give thanks to Thee for Thy great glory."

His particular love for the Feast of the Transfiguration can probably be explained by his many years of suffering. Father Paul knew that Christ gave to Peter, James, and John a glimpse of heaven on Tabor, and that for those who love and serve Christ and suffer with Him there is to come the joy of an everlasting Tabor, so beautifully expressed in the hymn of the First Vespers of the feast:

> *All you who seek, in hope and love*
> *For your dear Lord, look up above:*
> *Faith may a glorious form descry*
> *Lo! on the trembling verge of light*
> *We see something divinely bright,*
> *Immortal, infinite, sublime,*
> *Older than chaos, space or time.*

Father Paul conducted a perpetual novena to St. Anthony, whom he called "the Friars' Elder Brother." Each night he would read aloud the various petitions sent in and the names of the senders. Listed under the various requests were a long list of names. Father Paul kept reading a particular petition for months which always brought a smile over the faces of the community. After the petitions had been read for health, employment, lost articles, success in examination, he would look up at the image of St. Anthony and say, "and a husband for Nellie C." Finally, after praying for the request of "Nellie C." for months, Father Paul ended the list of petitions one night with the words, "and thanksgiving to St. Anthony for Nellie C. And now may she live happily ever after."

During the novena service he would speak with the complete simplicity and naïveté which were characteristic of his whole life. During the Depression years there was

Rooting for his baseball team: he hated to lose

always a long list of petitioners asking St. Anthony's prayers for employment. At the end of the list Father Paul would occasionally say, "And do not forget the ten million others who are unemployed." During this particular period when the friar in charge of the Administration Building was besieged by merchants who were insistent that food, coal, and clothing bills be paid, he went one day to Father Paul and told him that the bills now amounted to over 50,000 dollars. Father Paul's answer was, "Now, don't worry, for that is St. Anthony's job and he will see to it that the bills will be paid." "Well, Father," replied the priest, "I wish St. Anthony were here to answer the telephone and assure these insistent merchants of their money." Father Paul, with a beaming smile replete with faith and confidence, said: "I have him constantly on the heavenly telephone of prayer."

Pentecost Sunday in the year 1939 was a beautiful day. Thousands of pilgrims came to Graymoor. The afternoon devotions and the novena to St. Anthony were scheduled to be broadcast at three P.M. As usual Father Paul was to give the sermon. The large bell in St. Francis's chapel was rung and the people began to gather on the lawn. Father Paul sat under a tree making the usual last-minute revisions in his sermon. Suddenly a strong wind started to blow and increased in strength every minute. Toward the west the sky began to darken and great black thunderheads to accumulate. The sky over Graymoor became darker. Brother Aelred, who had charge of the St. Anthony Radio Hour, wondered if the storm would hold off until after the broadcast. He stepped up to the microphone and asked the pilgrims to say some prayers to St. Anthony, asking his intercessory prayers before the throne of God that the storm pass over Graymoor. In a few minutes the sky became blacker and the wind was roaring. Brother Aelred began to move the microphones under the trees in the hope that if the storm did break during the broadcast the organist and choir could fill in after Father Paul's sermon, for if it rained there would be no Benediction of the Most Blessed Sacrament. When he had moved the second microphone Father Paul's voice came over the public address system from another part of the lawn.

"Now, see here, Brother Aelred," he said, "that is not the way to show your faith in St. Anthony. You asked the pilgrims to pray for his help, and you are not waiting to find out if he is going to give a favorable answer."

Brother Aelred was embarrassed and apologized, moving the microphones back where they had been.

It was then five minutes to three, the hour the program was scheduled to go on the air. Having had experience in the field of radio before he became a friar, Brother Aelred judged that the best decision was to telephone the radio station in New York that the broadcast was off; but, in the light of what had happened, he did not dare.

Three o'clock came, with the sky over Graymoor getting darker and the wind now a heavy gale—and the Saint Anthony Hour went on the air. The pilgrims seemed nervous, and the novices singing the opening theme had one eye on the music and the other on the clouds, which were now black. As the announcer began to speak there came a sudden blinding flash of lightning that struck the water tower dedicated to the Holy Spirit. The radio engineer was lifted out of his chair and the thousands of pilgrims sat stunned. Then the thunder roared and the lightning flashed and the wind was so violent that it seemed the trees would be uprooted. Finally, the heavens opened and Graymoor was deluged with water. It seeemd as if the floods of Niagara were inundating the earth. The pilgrims scattered in all directions, the radio engineer made a hurried "sign-off" and dashed for shelter, the choir and organist ran for the nearest cover. In a few minutes thousands of people seemingly disappeared off the face of the earth. Brother Aelred stood in the downpour, dazed. He thought he was alone until he saw Father Paul under the tree, still revising his sermon. Then he went up to Father Paul and said: "I am afraid we cannot have the broadcast, Father."

With that gracious, benign smile that was so characteristic of him, Father Paul said: "No, I guess not. What Sunday is this, Brother Aelred?"

"Pentecost," said Brother Aelred.

"That's right; and the signs of the Holy Spirit are wind, fire, and water. We surely had the rushing of the wind, didn't we? And that lightning was certainly fire, wasn't it?" Then, stretching forth his hand in the heavy rain, he laughed and said: "We certainly cannot doubt the water, can we? Well, if the Holy Spirit wishes to show us His mighty signs on His great feast days, I guess, He can take precedence over our powerful St. Anthony to do so."

Father Paul and Brother Aelred walked in the teeming rain and, with soaked habits, entered the Little Flower chapel where hundreds of pilgrims found shelter. Laying aside his prepared radio sermon he gave an impromptu one on the Holy Spirit with all the beauty and magnificence of his gifted tongue.

It was in an impromptu sermon that Father Paul was at his best. The obligation that radio stations placed on him to submit his sermons for approval before a broadcast greatly irritated him. Before a broadcast, or during one in a New York studio, he would sit in a corner revising a sermon that had already been submitted and approved. When a friar companion would, with great tact, tell him that he was not permitted to change his sermon he would indignantly ask: "Who said so? Don't the radio people know yet that God owns the air waves, and that the radio is a gift out of God's storehouse of treasures so that men may learn of Him?" Often he was cautioned that he would be cut off the air if he changed his sermon again. His answer was always his usual benign smile; and the following Sunday the same thing would happen. Where the things of God were concerned no man intimidated Father Paul. Had he lived under a persecutor of the Church he would have been among the martyrs.

X

Onward Christian Soldiers

IT WAS 5 A.M. AND FATHER PAUL rose from the straw-filled mattress in his tiny cell at the friary to put on his habit and begin another day packed with the activities to which by 1935 he had long been accustomed. Hardly had he finished dressing, however, when his friar secretary rushed into the room to announce that he was urgently needed down at the convent. Bring the holy oils for anointing of the sick, the secretary advised. Father Paul instinctively knew what the matter was without being told.

For years now, and increasingly so in the past few months, he had watched helplessly as his beloved cofounder succumbed to the ravages of the cancer that was eating her away. Her hands crippled by severe arthritis, her throat most of the time constricted by the spreading melanoma to the point where she could not even take water, her skin a mass of ulceratered sores caused by erysipelas, Mother Lurana had gamely and bravely tried to go about her regular routine during the first few months of 1935. Despite her illness, which she knew was terminal, the foundress supervised the establishment of a number of new convents for her community both in America and abroad. Nonetheless, her attempts at preserving normality had been interrupted by frequent trips to the hospital, long periods of isolated rest at the community's summer villa in Long Beach, New York, and even more protracted absences from regular community functions.

During the first two weeks of April 1935 she grew steadily weaker and became almost comatose. "It is pathetic," her secretary wrote, "to see Mother so ill and we helpless to aid her, but she is so edifying and resigned to her heavy cross."

Rushing down the hill to the convent, Father Paul found Mother Lurana dying and in severe pain. After administering the anointing of the sick, he left her room about 6:10 A.M. to celebrate the liturgy for the sisters' community. No sooner had he reached the sacristy than the sister nurse called him back. This was the end. Reciting the prayers for the dying, Father Paul eased his coworker of many years out of her earthly existence into the final unity which she so much desired. It was Monday of Holy Week, April 1935, nearly 65 years from the date of her birth in another Holy Week, 1870.

While removing the Mother's few, small possessions, one of the sisters found in her desk a final testament to her community which read: "Dearest Daughters, I charge each and every one of you—give to the newly elected Mother the same loyalty and obedience that you have ever given to me. Love and obey all set over you. Keep charity among yourselves as dear Sisters in the Atonement. Ever keep closely united with the Motherhouse. Hate and abhor the spirit of criticism which leads to separations and divisions. Be ever faithful children of the church. . . ." She ended by giving her blessing to all and asked for their continual prayers.

On Wednesday, April 17, the Mother Foundress was buried within the outdoor shrine of Our Lady of the Atonement on the convent grounds. At the liturgy preceding the burial, Monsignor Louis Lavelle, vicar general of the archdiocese, preached a eulogy of the Foundress, using as his text the words from the Book of Proverbs: "Who shall find a valiant woman. Far and from the farthest cost is the price of her." For Father Paul, this was to be his first Easter Sunday in over 35 years without the physical presence of his faithful collaborator in the great work of making Christians at-one. Rightfully Mother Lurana may be called a "handmaid of Christian unity," just as Father Paul had often said she was the "handmaid of *The Lamp*." In a letter to members of the Rosary League one month later, Paul wrote of the Foundress:

Having the name of the Atonement she was called by God to be an atoning victim in union with the Crucified. At the commencement of her religious life she saw herself as a slain lamb and this vision of the night was particularly fulfilled in her last long illness extending over many months, during which time to an extraordinary and striking degree she was conformed to the image of the Lamb slain upon the cross. Unable to take food or drink without experiencing great nausea, she passed through a long period of fasting almost as absolute as that of Our Lord in the wilderness. She once spoke of her body as a "pain factory" and truly such it was. For a time one particular part of the body would be subjected to excruciating pain; and when it became almost unendurable it suddenly shifted to some other portion of the body, until almost every organ or member was involved in the sufferings of the crucified. . . .

Indicative of Father Paul's appreciation of Mother Lurana and her significance for his own career as an apostle of unity was his rather questionable practice, after her death, of encouraging a quasi-cultic devotion to the foundress among friends of Graymoor. There are frequent references in his correspondence like this: "Mother Lurana left a letter to be read after her transitus and in it she said: 'If our Lord permits, and I think He will, I will help you and the Institute after my death; therefore think of me as not far off,' and we do feel her invisible presence among us, particularly here at the Convent where I am dictating this letter. She has done many wonderful things for the communities since her departure." Later, he remarked that "Mother Lurana is being invoked by an increasing number of faithful Catholics who keep on sending us testimonials of prayers she has graciously answered." Even as late as the spring of 1938 he was writing to an inquirer: "I regret that the Friars or Sisters of the Atonement have never composed a special prayer to be addressed to Mother Lurana. It is something we must take care of in the near future. . . . I am sending you one of Mother Foundress' Requiem cards together with a picture of Our Lady of the Atonement and I would recommend you to address the latter, calling at the same time upon Mother Lurana in your own words to obtain that which you seek." Father Paul's unwise fostering of such unauthorized devotions, of course, eventually came to the attention of archdiocesan officials.

Others sorrows awaited him. At that time, early in 1939, the community of friars was on the brink of bankruptcy, due mainly to Paul's unflagging charity to the poor and needy to the neglect of providing for a sound financial base at home. Add to this the continuing suspicions among some bishops and clergy about Graymoor being still "Protestant" or being headed by wide-eyed visionaries, and it is apparent how vulnerable Father Paul was to the demands of the authorities in New York. Further difficulties were not long in coming. At the helm of the Archiodiocese of New York was Archbishop Francis Spellman, and his chancellor was Monsignor James Francis McIntyre. Both were known for their talents at financial administration in a day of "brick and mortar" churchmanship; both eventually became cardinals of the Roman Church. Of the two, McIntyre was perhaps the more financially adept, having come to a career in the Church after years of experience on Wall Street.

Perhaps the last straw for the archdiocese came when news arrived from abroad that Father Paul, in attempting to fulfill a favorite project of his, the establishment of a house of his congregation in Rome as a sign of his fidelity to the pope, had somehow run afoul of the intricate currency regulations required by the Italian government. Complaints came to the Vatican, already jittery over unsettled conditions in Europe, and the frantic order went out for the immediate end of Father Paul's transactions at any cost.

Since there are few documents available to reveal

exactly what happened, and reliance on oral testimony from friars acquainted with the situation is risky at best, perhaps the most accurate account of the founder's last difficulties in 1939 is found in the written, though unpublished, recollections of the friar who served as Father Paul's personal chauffeur at the time.

Undoubtedly one of the most difficult days in the life of Father Paul occurred in November 1939. At the request of Monsignor McIntyre, who at that time was Chancellor of the Archdiocese of New York, Archbishop Spellman summoned Father Paul to be at the Ordinary's house at 2 P.M. on the following day and to bring with him the treasurer. Father Vicar went with us. We were on time, and so was the Archbishop. It was a stormy session. We could not have a parish in Rome. The 20,000 dollars we had there in trust with the Cardinal Vicar of Rome was to be returned immediately. Fr. Valentine Snyder was introduced. And we were told that Father Snyder was to be a personal representative of His Excellency with residence at Graymoor, and furthermore that we were a diocesan community and that the Archbishop of New York had authority from the Holy See to completely suppress the Society of the Atonement if and when in his opinion that was advisable. The Archbishop went on to say that if we wanted to make the possibility of suppression known it was up to us, that he was telling no one except us. . . . After the meeting was over, Father Vicar went somewhere, and Father Snyder went somewhere else. I got the car and picked up Father General at 452 Madison Avenue, and when we got to the West Side Highway I said: "There isn't much to talk about." He answered: "There is a whole lot to talk about," but there was not another word spoken by either of us on the way to Graymoor. At the Convent, Father General got out, where I suppose he had a very light supper. In my whole life I have never felt more sorry for anyone.

Clearly Father Paul and the society were in grave trouble. Indeed, a whole lifetime's work was in danger of collapse and the ecumenical apostolate of the community was threatened as never before. How exceedingly fragile was the whole enterprise after nearly 40 years of hard work, devotion, and generosity to others. Indeed, Father Paul was in difficulty from the very beginning to the end of his career in the Roman Church. To be fair, however, it must be remembered that he fared no better as an Anglican. In retrospect, one can understand how uncomfortable Father Paul made the archdiocesan officials in New York. Accustomed to acceptable financial procedures, the authorities were no doubt aghast at Paul's unusual fund-raising gimmicks and his repeated failure to keep his accounts in the black. It must, therefore, have been a very sad Christmas that year for Father Paul, his last on this earth.

Only three months after his meeting with the archdiocesan officials in New York, Father Paul awakened in the middle of the night, Thursday, February 8, 1940, with a severe pain in his chest. He told the brother infirmarian whom he had roused from sleep that one of his arms was numb and he felt nauseated. In the quiet of the night a priest was called as was a physician resident at Graymoor. Each did his duty by Father Paul, who was in very severe pain. Shortly after 4 A.M., however, the sisters at the bottom of the hill were awakened an hour earlier than usual by the haunting toll of bells in the darkness. The phone rang in the Mother General's office, and her secretary returned with the word that the founder had been pronounced dead at 4 A.M., a few minutes before.

All over America, radio stations broadcast the announcement of Paul's death in brief lines like these: "In the foothills of the Catskills at Graymoor, Garrison, New

York, the Catholic Church in America has today suffered a great loss. There, in a monastery, died a famous Franciscan friar, Father Paul James Francis. He was an international leader in Church affairs. As the Founder of the Society of the Atonement his work among the poor was known throughout the world." From everywhere in the United States and Canada as well as from around the world messages of condolence and appreciation poured into Graymoor. The editor of the *Catholic Courier*, newspaper of the Roman Catholic diocese of Rochester, New York, said it perhaps as well as any when he wrote: "With the death of Father Paul James Francis came the close of a career most interesting and most unique. So devoted to the ideals of the religious life was this man that he moved among the people of this generation as an almost medieval figure. He sought for the light and he found it through God's grace. He heard the call of divine vocation and he answered it. . . . The Church Unity Octave, observed throughout the world as a time of special prayer and devotion for the reunion of all Christians in the true faith, was the inspiration of Father Paul, and may be the accomplishment around which will center the most lasting memories of his life. . . . While we pray for the soul of Father Paul, let us try to match his zeal for the Church of God!"

On Monday, February 12th, 1940, the friars and sisters of the Atonement laid to rest the body of their founder in a small, musty crypt beneath the superstructure of the still unfinished "great shrine" that Father Paul had begun so long ago.

Gradually the society stabilized itself financially in the years after Father Paul's death. This was due to the hard work of the officials and members of the community, all of

The final years

whom began to realize more fully what it was that Father Paul had accomplished. They discovered that it took at least 100 friars to do what Paul had achieved almost alone. Because Father Paul had been nearly a one-man show, few of the members, most of whom were in training for the apostolate until his death, realized the full scope of the society's commitments, financial and otherwise. But the friars were eventually equal to the charge. One thing that they never did complete was the "great shrine" of Father Paul. Over the years the ravages of weather and continued abuse made Paul's "great shrine" a hazard, good for nothing but storage. Standing like some huge Gothic castle burned out by fire, the "great shrine" today looms out over the valley below, brooding upon its sad fate as a visible reminder of his unfinished dreams. This struck some modern-day friars as a quite inappropriate site for the tomb of Father Paul.

Years later the casket of the founder was moved out of that dank cellar and reburied on the top of the Mount of the Atonement overlooking the beautiful Hudson Valley which he loved so much. Beneath a resplendent white statue of Michelangelo's Pieta, the site of reburial is marked by a large granite slab inscribed with the founder's name, the dates of his life, and the words: That All May Be One. On October 9th, 1971, the date of reburial, several hundred friars, sisters, clergy, and friends gathered to honor the founder once more and to renew their own spirit of At-one-ment.

Leading the Roman Catholic *and* Anglican rites were the Very Reverend Michael Daniel, S.A., the Father General of the society, the Most Reverend Joseph Pernicone, Roman Catholic Auxiliary Bishop of New York, and the Right Reverend J. Stuart Wetmore, Suffragan Bishop of the Episcopal Diocese of New York. Commenting on the event, Bishop Wetmore said in part: "How wonderful it was that you moved the body of Brother Paul out of that crumbling and decaying building and placed it beneath God's green earth with His glorious sky above. That unfinished building is a symbol of death. But Graymoor is not crumbling. The horizon of the friars is broad and creative. This new tomb site is symbolic of your wide vision." In identifying Father Paul with the virtue of Christian faith, Father Daniel encouraged his listeners to strengthen their own faith so that their efforts in the ecumenical apostolate might have the same firm base as that of the founders. Indeed, he continued, "this day we honor not only Father Paul but also Mother Lurana. They cannot be separated. There was no problem of 'women's liberation' or 'man's supremacy' with this God-inspired couple. They believed they were called by God, not individually, but together to do the work of the Lord."

Between the death of Father Paul in 1940 and the reburial of his body in 1971, momentous changes occurred in the world and in the Churches. As a product of both world and Church, the Society of the Atonement naturally reflected in itself most of these developments. Despite the fact of a World War, a worldwide economic recession, and the involvement of the United States in a "military action" in Korea, the 1940s and 1950s were years of relatively great expansion and growth for the Churches. They were, moreover, a time of organizational rigidity, doctrinal certainty, and institutional isolation for Roman Catholics, in the United States particularly. As a largely American phenomenon, therefore, the society also portrayed many of these qualities.

During this period the community grew threefold in

numbers alone, from less than 100 to nearly 300 members. Financially, it developed a solid base for expansion under the adept leadership of two different Fathers General. No longer did the society live from hand to mouth as in the days of Father Paul. A large minor seminary was opened in 1949 at Montour Falls, New York, to continue that tradition of educating young boys for the priesthood, which had been begun by Father Paul when he opened St. John's Seminary at Graymoor. In Washington, D.C., a new building was constructed in 1952 to provide accommodations for the large number of friar seminarians studying at the Catholic University of America. The old Robinson mansion was no longer sufficient. At Cumberland, Rhode Island, a former Trappist monastery that had been partially destroyed by fire was renovated in 1951 as a novitiate for the young men who were jamming St. Joseph's building for postulants at Graymoor and the old novitiate at Saranac Lake, New York. Near the end of the 1950s plans were being drawn for the construction at Graymoor of a multimillion dollar seminary and friary which was opened in 1960 as St. Piux X Seminary.

Educationally friar priests were being trained in various specialties at major Roman Catholic universities in the United States and abroad. Eventually the society had an educational system which was staffed almost entirely by highly qualified friars and which ranged from the first year of high school, through college, to the program in theology. Given the number of personnel available for that purpose and the immense cost of providing facilities and faculties, this was a major accomplishment for the small society.

Besides maintaining the St. Christopher's Inn, the Graymoor Press, *The Lamp*, the Ave Maria Hour, and the original mission parishes at Hereford, Texas; Vancouver, British Columbia; and Kinston, North Carolina, the society began to set its sights both outside North America and beyond the South of the United States.

Elsewhere on the North American continent additional parishes and centers were opened in North Carolina among the black people, in Western Canada among foreign seamen and native Indians, and in Eastern Canada where a large retreat center was established at Gardiner Mines, Nova Scotia. Abroad, the friars assumed control of the Church of St. Onofrio on the Janiculum Hill in Rome, Italy, and during 1949 the first members departed for a large mission territory in the diocese of Yokohama, Japan. In the early 1960s the community established another mission in the diocese of Goias, Brazil. A few years earlier the friars had taken charge of the large Catholic Central Library in London, England. Certainly the Children of the Atonement were growing rapidly, even beyond the most extravagant dreams of Father Paul. Optimism, confidence, certainty, progress were signs of the times. In effect, there was a religious bull market.

Ecumenically, of course, the stance among most members of the society was still one of a ghettoized, fortress mentality as it was in the Roman Church of the day and as it had also been in the time of Father Paul. Insular and defensive, the Roman Church issued a monitum in 1948, for example, which warned Roman Catholics that they were forbidden to participate in "mixed congresses of Catholics and non-Catholics" and "without leave of the Holy See." Coming as it did on June 5th, a few days before the opening of the meeting at Amsterdam, Netherlands, which gave birth to the World Council of Churches, the monitum of the Holy Office was a deliberate attempt to discourage any Roman participation in that assembly, or any other like it for that matter.

During 1949 an Instruction of the Holy Office, called *Ecclesia Catholica*, further extended the prohibitions when it stated: "The Catholic Church takes no actual part in 'ecumenical' conventions and other assemblies of a similar character. Yet . . . she has, despite this fact never ceased nor will she ever cease to pursue with deepest concern and promote with assiduous prayers to God every endeavor to bring about what was so close to the heart of Christ the Lord, namely, that all who believe in Him 'may be made perfect in one.' " There is absolutely no ambiguity in the Instruction. The unity that is meant is the unity of the Roman Catholic Church, and reunion requires the acceptance of Roman Catholicism by non-Roman Christians. Naturally, individual conversion was conceived as the key to the accomplishment of Christian unity.

Among the friars this mentality and attitude was prevalent, as can be seen merely from reading the pages of *The Lamp* and the numerous pamphlets issued for the observance of the Chair of Unity Octave. Moreover, the friars vigorously promoted a correspondence course of religious instruction for those interested in the Roman Church and conducted a mission band which attempted not only to reclaim any "fallen-aways" from the Roman Church but also to bring into the Church as many non-Romans as possible. Convert instructions were very popular at the time and the friars responded to the demand.

Even in mission areas the friars concentrated their efforts chiefly on strengthening the walls of the Roman Catholic ghetto without much outreach toward non-Roman

Catholics and non-Christians or any cooperation in less strictly religious, more social projects of a community-wide nature. In fairness, however, it must be said that no individual friar or even the community at large can be faulted for having this narrow ecumenical vision. There were precious few at the time in the Roman Church who were doing *anything* at all that could be termed even vaguely ecumenical. Rather, the society reflected, sometimes all too forcefully, the socio-religious atmosphere within which it operated during the 1940s and 1950s.

The 1960s came as a shock to everyone, even to the Churches. Upheaval, rapid change, confusion, uncertainty, aimlessness, all became quite familiar to those who lived through that decade. For the Churches this was an extremely trying period of adaptation, readjustment and re-evaluation. In the Roman Church the Second Vatican Council, begun by good Pope John XXIII, offered trauma to some in the Church; to others it provided an opportunity for renewal and *aggiornamento*, the like of which had not been experienced since the time of the so-called Counter Reformation. Though long in coming, the renewal had its roots in the liturgical, theological, and biblical movements which had existed within the Church during the course of the previous 50 years or more. The Council in most cases merely concretized and authorized that which had already occurred quietly among small and often disparate groups in the Church. Elsewhere the story of this period in the Roman Church has been more than adequately told.

By no means was the Society of the Atonement left unaffected by these currents and movements in the Roman Church. Take only the matter of religious life-style, for example. Gone were the 5 A.M. rising, the constant wearing of the religious habit, the forced attendance at liturgical exercises, the unquestioning obedience due to superiors, the prohibitions against the use of alcohol and tobacco, the limitations on personal relationships between the sexes, the restrictions on travel and recreation. How uncomfortable Father Paul would truly have been had he lived into this era, because he was essentially a strict constructionist in his attitudes toward both the relgious life and the common morality.

Moreover, physically, apostolically, and ecumenically there were also drastic changes in the society during the 1960s. Hit by decreased giving among Roman Catholics and an ever-rising inflation, the society became far more cost-conscious than ever before. While by no means insolvent, the community now had to cover deficits in annual operating costs by tapping reserves and using large gifts that would ordinarily have been invested. Budgets were instituted, and a strict financial accounting of every friary and department was demanded. A moratorium on any construction of new buildings was called, and every friar was urged to tighten his belt. Sadly, one of the criteria for ceasing or initiating apostolic works was finances. The days of milk and honey which had begun in the early 1950s were almost at an end for the friars.

Numerically, the society held its own in the 1960s although it nonetheless suffered its share of departures from the priesthood and the religious life. Moreover, the great stream of vocations which the community was privileged to have in the 1940s and 1950s now declined. One of the more significant developments was that the society went completely out of the business of educating its own men. No longer were faculty members trained for the friars' own schools. Indeed what was built in the 50s was often closed in the 60s. At Montour Falls the minor seminary was terminated and the building sold to the State of New York. After seven short years of existence at Graymoor, the St. Pius X Seminary, which had earned the right to grant its own A.B. degree, ceased operations.

Though students still resided at Atonement Seminary in Washington, the faculty was disbanded and the young men were sent once again to the Catholic University and other neighboring schools. As an admissions policy it was required that every young man, whether he wished to be a brother or a priest, have a bachelor's degree in the liberal arts before entrance into the novitiate. Further, the massive acreage and buildings at the novitiate in Cumberland, Rhode Island, were sold to the local town, and the novitiate was moved into rented quarters at Medford, Massachusetts. All this in ten years. The pace of change was almost breathtaking.

In the field of the apostolate the society also experienced rapid developments. When high costs of paper and printing made any idea of a profitable operation impossible, the Graymoor Press went out of business. In the late 1960s the Ave Maria Hour made its last broadcast, and by the early 1970s *The Lamp* magazine was extinguished after more than 70 years of publication.

On the foreign missions of Japan and Brazil, stress was given to increased ecumenical involvement by the friars in the Land of the Rising Sun and to the various social aspects of pre-evangelization in South America. At home, friars became strongly committed to work with local ecumenical agencies in social projects, with ministerial associations and community organizations. As a policy it was

determined that the community would not assume charge
of any new parishes or centers unless there was clear opportunity for specifically ecumenical activities. Because there
were evident needs not being met by the state in the areas
of alcoholic rehabilitation and drug abuse, the work of St.
Christopher's Inn was expanded by opening St. Joseph's
Rehabilitation Center for alcoholic men in Saranac Lake,
New York and the New Hope Manor at Graymoor for
young women with drug problems.

Ecumenically, the community still bore its share of the
burden. In fact its central purpose for existence, the ecumenical apostolate, was rediscovered. Besides publishing
the monthly *Ecumenical Trends* and the quarterly *Conver-
sations,* the society developed an ecumenical retreat and
conference facility, the Graymoor Christian Unity Center,
in the building which formerly housed St. Pius X Seminary.
At the center, conferences, days of recollection, informal
and organized retreats are held for Christians of every
denomination or none. In addition to its regular quarterly
conferences on ecumenical topics and its sponsorship of
the Week of Prayer for Christian Unity in the United
States, the Graymoor Ecumenical Institute has organized
the Ecumenical Clergy Associates, a body of committed
clergy who encourage one another in the ecumenical apostolate on the local level. The Associates is a so-called "grass
roots" group of those who wish to share their ideas and
concerns in ecumenism and who might otherwise become
isolated and discouraged by the apathy and ignorance of
others. The friars fulfilled the dream of Father Paul by
expanding their ecumenical work at their *Centro pro
Unione* in downtown Rome and at the Catholic Central
Library in London. His friars now labor both in Rome, the

City of Peter, and in England, "Mary's dowry," the birth-
place of the Anglican communion.

Periodically, the Graymoor Ecumenical Institute, the
chief ecumenical organ of the society, presents the Father
Paul Christian Unity Award to honor individuals who have
made major ecumenical contributions in the Churches.
Among its recipients have been Augustine Cardinal Bea,
Lawrence Cardinal Shehan, Dr. Martin E. Marty, and
recently the Anglican-Roman Catholic International Commission which has issued some stated agreements on the
Eucharist and ministry that would have warmed the heart
of Father Paul. But the recipient of the Christian Unity
Award who would really have brought great joy to Father
Paul was duly honored on the evening of January 26th,
1972.

On that day in the large Martin Luther King Room of
the Graymoor Christian Unity Center a crowd of friars,
sisters, clergy, and friends gave a rousing welcome to His
Grace, Arthur Michael Ramsey, Archbishop of Canterbury
and Primate of All England. Besides friars and sisters of the
society, those invited to participate in the historic event
were Bishop Joseph Pernicone, the local Roman Catholic
vicar, Bishop J. Stuart Wetmore of the New York Episcopal diocese, local Roman Catholic and Episcopal clergy,
and the ecumenical commissions of both dioceses. Following the presentation of the award by the Father General
of the society, Very Reverend Michael Daniel, S.A., the
Archbishop of Canterbury made some informal remarks in
which he said in part:

Let me share with you my conviction, which I'm quite certain
is your conviction also, that the secret of unity is renewal.

Renewal spiritual, renewal intellectual, and renewal in Christian life and mission. And I believe that perhaps the most signal service of the beloved Pope John XXIII to Christendom was his great witness to the linking of unity with renewal. Not trying to negotiate how we can bring our Churches together just as they are but how we can change and reform and reshape our own Church life through being renewed in Christ, in holiness, in truth and in the Christian faith. And as this process of renewal in Christ goes on among Roman Catholics and goes on among Anglicans, we are digging down, digging down in greater spiritual depths to a kind of plane where unity in Christ is found. This renewal includes, first of all, the renewal in prayer and in the contemplation of God. It carries with it the intellectual renewal of theological truth, what Pope Paul and I described in our common declarations as seeking unity based upon the holy Gospels and ancient common traditions. By the deepening of our apprehension of the mystery of God in Christ, by a deeper exploring of that mystery, we find ourselves closer together.

After the award ceremonies the archbishop and Mrs. Ramsey went out with the Father General of the society into the bright night to pray at the tomb of Father Paul. The lights of New York City were visible from that lovely spot as the 100th successor of St. Augustine raised both hands in prayer. Father Paul and Mother Lurana would have rejoiced to be there. Who can say that they were not?

So ends the story of Father Paul of Graymoor, who attempted in his own person to unite what were in his own day warring camps. His vision of a united Christendom caused him for a while to be a pro-papal Anglican, and then a Roman Catholic concerned for the reunion of the Churches.

Like all dreamers he looked forward to a goal which

seemed impossible in his own day. His views exposed him to constant persecution and misunderstanding. It is providential that from his earliest years he was devoted to the Cross.

Many of his projects, like the magazine he founded and the seminaries he built, are a thing of the past. They served their purpose in their day and have given way to other developments in the life of the Church. Yet there is so much of permanence in the witness of his life.

By sheer persistence in his propagation of the Week of Prayer for Christian Unity he perhaps accomplished more than anyone else in holding ecumenical ideals before the eyes of Roman Catholics in the days before Pope John, when everything outside the visible confines of that Church was viewed with xenophobic suspicion. He helped Roman Catholics to appreciate in some small way the agony of the divisions that separated them from their brother Christians of other Churches and communities. In a very real way he prepared the ground for the tremendous ecumenical revolution which took place in the Roman Catholic Church under the guidance and inspiration of Pope John XXIII. At least he made his fellow Roman Catholics aware that there were Churches other than their own, no matter how imperfect in their eyes.

To those Christians who were not of the Roman Church he held aloft his papal banner with courage and fierce determination. In an age of fanatical bigotry he dared to suggest that the question of Roman primacy was central to any serious consideration of Christian reunion. He never lived to see the day when theologians of various Churches could at least discuss the possible need for a universal ministry of visible unity to the whole Church of

God, the possibility that a renewed papacy in an ecumenical age might serve as the focal point for the reunion of sister Churches in the one Communion of Christ.

His evangelical simplicity, expressed in his devotion to his vow of poverty, was not only a rebuke to a materialistic age but a vision of commitment for contemporary society, which experiences a spiritual vacuum in the midst of technological affluence. To spend the minimum on self so that one could give the maximum to others, to use all of one's time, talent, substance, and opportunity for God and others is an inspiration for our day of spiritual starvation.

His vision of reconciliation, which runs through all of his thoughts, words, and actions, gives coherence to a life filled with a multitude of projects and a pluralism of responses to immediate problems. To make all men at one with God, at one with each other, at one even with themselves was the driving force that caused him to argue for the visible unity of Christians as a vision that would inspire all mankind. To reach out to those in need abroad, to receive poor homeless men at his own doorstep, to heal their wounds and to reintegrate them into universal human fellowship under God was his burning passion.

He was like some saintly showman, a Gothic Barnum whose limitless enthusiasm, fiery courage, and grand vision surmounted seemingly endless obstacles. He had no time for anything else but his cause of unity. His life is like a straight arrow, pointing in only one direction. He knew how to reach masses of people and communicate the spark of his vision. Sometimes his heart overcame his head and he got into trouble.

In the last month of his life, with the threat of the suppression of his religious community hanging over his head, he went to Washington, D.C., for what was to be his last appearance away from Graymoor. He was no more secure then, as he stood in the pulpit of the National Shrine of the Immaculate Conception, than he had been almost half a century before when he started. What was he to say on this occasion, the work of his life hanging in the balance, the Society of the Atonement itself living from day to day under the shadow of financial insolvency and ecclesiastical censure? Had it all been worth it? Would he have done it all had he known what he knew now?

Those who heard him that January of 1940 remember the sermon well. It was the same sermon he preached in his Anglican days on Long Island so many years before. "Silver and gold have I none, but such as I have I give unto Thee, in the name of Jesus Christ of Nazareth, rise up and walk." It was the story of the lame man at the Temple gate from the Book of Acts, and he said again at the end of his ministry what he had said at its beginning 40 years before. God had a plan of reconciliation and unity for all mankind. Paul's vision of that plan might not be shared by everyone, but one could only admire his steadfast devotion to that ideal.

Although he died in uncertainty, his great life's work, the Society of the Atonement, survives to this day, enjoying a rejuvenated commitment to the ideals of its founder as reconfirmed and further expanded by Pope John. His work goes on despite discouragement and difficulties.

While Father Paul was Roman Catholic in loyalty and doctrine, the evangelical ethos of his witness frequently struck an unexpectedly ecumenical note. Our favorite picture of him is contained in his reminiscences of the Holy Year pilgrimage he made to Rome in 1925 as the leader of a group of pilgrims. Having made their rounds of the holy places, they came at last to the Vatican.

Last in order, but first in importance, we visited Saint Peter's. Grouped about the Altar erected above the tomb of the Vicar of Christ we sung (*sic*) "Holy God, We Praise Thy Name," while hundreds standing about listened with evident pleasure; and then having said the Jubilee Prayers, we circled the Confessional, as it is called, singing lustily with splendid effect: "Onward Christian Soldiers."

Perhaps all of this is best summed up by John Cardinal Willebrands, President of the Vatican's Secretariat for the Promotion of Christian Unity, when he said: "Not even Father Paul was fully aware of the implications of the ideals which he pursued, but the promptings of the Spirit are always deeper than we are able to understand."

Anglican and Roman Catholic rites mark the re-intombment of Father Paul at Graymoor in 1971